Death From Child Abuse...
and no one heard

"There's rarely been a more affecting and impassioned plea on behalf of children. Highly recommended for professionals, parents, and anyone who cares about children."

Child Welfare League of America, Inc.

"Our office has recommended to the training coordinating agencies that *Death From Child Abuse...and no one heard* be read by all the instructors teaching our state's mandated 20-hour Child Care Training Course. This book clearly demonstrates and reinforces the need for all individuals working with children to become actively involved in preventing child abuse."

Larry Pintacuda, Program Supervisor
State of Florida
Department of Health and Rehabilitative Services

"At a time when some are questioning the need to protect children because of fears of "intrusions" into family, this book compellingly documents one of the thousands of child abuse cases that occur in the United States yearly. Child protection is a high priority...child abuse deaths will continue. Read this book and then get involved in preventing abuse deaths in your community."

Richard D. Krugman, M.D.
Dean, University of Colorado School of Medicine

"I can think of no more effective means of alerting people to the tragedy of child abuse than by making this book available to teachers, pastors, doctors, nurses, and parents across the country. By making those who work with children and families aware of the enormity of this problem, the war on child abuse can be won."

Alice MacMahon
Director, The Center for Women's Medicine
Florida Hospital

"What a compelling book. The account of the last days of Ursula Sunshine Assaid is shocking, it makes one hurt and then angry. Angry enough to want to do something so that no other child would have to undergo such torturous treatment."

Lt. Sam Flanigan
Salvation Army

"This is a book you will not enjoy reading. This story makes an excellent start on enlarging awareness of the problem by presenting one terrible tragedy as historical fiction. It may sicken or repulse you. It may enrage you. But it will affect you. I strongly recommend that anyone involved in the care of children, indeed, anyone who cares about children, should read this book, as painful and discomforting as it will be. Children are being abused and neglected at this moment. Children are crying, right now. We must have the courage to hear."

Kay Holt, M.D.
Practicing Child Psychiatrist

"Thank you for letting me preview this book. This is a most important book, because it tells in a graphic and vivid manner the story of the last few days in the life of a bright happy little girl who was tortured and finally killed in the guise of discipline. The voice of Ursula Assaid, like that of Wendy Johnson, Corey Greer, Lisa Steinberg and many other children was not heard during life, but Ursula, at least will be heard now.

Norman Boyd
Parents Anonymous of Florida, Inc.

"Reading Death From Child Abuse...and no one heard, made me angry that there is still so much that needs to be done to protect the innocent victims. I am constantly looking for methods to bring this issue to the forefront of public concern and will include your book in the "must read" category."

Ken Eikenberry
Attorney General of Washington

"I wish I could say that Death From Child Abuse...and no one heard was a rare example of the plight of child abuse victims. Unfortunately, Ursula Sunshine Assaid was a victim of society-wide lack of understanding and concern for our most vulnerable citizens—our children. If everyone in our society was forced to read this chronicle we would stand a better chance of finally and conclusively recognizing the significance of abuse and exploitation of our youngest citizens.

Jay Howell
Executive Director
National Center for Missing and Exploited Children

Death From Child Abuse...
and no one heard

Death From Child Abuse
...and no one heard

Eve Krupinski and Dana Weikel

Edited by John G. Cronin

Currier Davis Publishing
Gulfport, Florida

For more information and to order additional copies of this book please call (727) 327-9039 or visit the website:
www.deathfromchildabuse.com

Printed in the United States of America

First Printing	1986
Second Printing	1988
Third Printing	1990
Fourth Printing & Revision	1999
Fifth Printing Revised and Updated	2002

 ISBN 0-930507-04-5

Requests to use any of the material contained herein may be emailed to: pub@deathfromchildabuse.com
or mailed to:

Currier Davis Publishing
4791 Baywood Point Drive S.
Gulfport, FL 33711
PH: 727-327-9039
FAX: 727-323-9587

website: www.deathfromchildabuse.com

Foreword

This year in the United States over one million children
will be reported as abused. The real numbers are probably many
times the reported cases. Two thousand children will die from
abuse. Child Abuse has an impact on our society that is
staggering. Maltreated children have an 84 percent failure rate
in school. Their drug dependency rates approach 70 percent,
and a high incidence of retardation is found in these child
victims.

Prison surveys indicate that 90 percent of the prison
population have been victims of child abuse. Various studies
indicate that between 70 and 90 percent of those in prison for
sexual offenses were themselves sexually victimized as
children. The research is clear that abusing parents were often
themselves abused. This is particularly so with males. Quite
often the target child becomes victimized at the same age when
the parent was first abused.

In a study of 200 prostitutes, 70 percent indicated that sexual
exploitation of them as children led to their subsequent
involvement as prostitutes. The current research shows that
sexual abuse of girls exceeds the previously thought number of
one out of every ten girls as victims. There are long-term
psychic scars that affect self image, profession, marriage,
divorce, the family and our society as a whole.

Judge Walter Komanski
Ninth Judicial Circuit Court
State of Florida

Acknowledgements

Without the assistance of the following people, we would not have found the stamina or heart to complete Ursula's story.

Melanie Arrington – our liaison with the Foundation

Andy & Cindy Weikel – our "coffee bearers."

George Weikel – for original lunch treats.

Brandon Weikel – for allowing us to cuddle and hug him when the story became too much…(a lot to ask of a five-month-old baby).

Joseph Krupinski – for patience and understanding.

John Cronin – for his expert hand in editing and his steadfast patience with the authors.

Christine Crosby and Judy Fontenot – for their faith in us as authors and their belief in the need for Ursula's story to be told, and to others who would go unnamed by their own choice, but to all, thank you!

Eve Krupinski
Dana Weikel

We are most grateful to the following individuals for their contributions to Part Two:

Jonathan H. Vanden, The Spring of Tampa Bay,

Sgt. Stephanie Campbell, Pinellas County Sheriff's Office

Meredith Bowman, St. Petersburg College

David Akullian, N. Berkeley Center for Family Counseling

Dr. Martha Coulter, University of South Florida

Jonathan B. Micocci, Executive Editor

Publisher

Table of Contents

Dedication

Perhaps it was a day like this; a rainy, balmy day when you first cried in pain. Perhaps it was a sunny day when happy children like to sing in swings; tumble down grassy banks, laughing and experiencing the freshness of life when the darkness we call "child abuse" crept into your life. Whenever it was, wherever it was, Ursula, we were not there. We were too late to hear your cry for help – you were too young to know that we cared, too young to know that you could reach out to us. We hear your cries now as the story of those terrible 55 hours unfolds. It is so painful to picture that life of a beautiful little girl being destroyed. You must have been very frightened and cold, Ursula, standing naked into the night. You must have been very tired and hungry, but worst of all, you must have felt abandoned by all of us. To know the agony, humiliation, intimidation and other abuse you suffered before you gave in to death made me angry. Angry that our society sleeps while other young children, like yourself, suffer. That we did not hear you, nor see the sadness in your eyes, nor sense your anxiety, brings us shame. You had no spokesperson for life. For that Ursula, we are sorry.

Phyllis Stopford

Introduction

The body of five-year-old Ursula Sunshine Assaid was recovered from a shallow drainage pond in Altamonte Springs, Florida, on December 1, 1982. She died at her home of the night of September 25, 1982, following two months of continuous abuse which ended in 55 hours of torture.

On June 16, 1983, Susan Assaid pleaded guilty to manslaughter in the death of her daughter and was sentenced to 15 years in prison.

On November 4, 1983, Donald McDougall was sentenced to 34 years in prison for the second degree murder conviction resulting from the brutal torture and abuse of Ursula Sunshine Assaid.

Ursula was described as a happy, bright child full of life and a delight to be around. She was well behaved, outgoing, and rarely into trouble. She laughed a lot, and was exceptionally friendly to almost everyone. She loved stuffed animals and had a bedroom full of them. She was a normal child who loved her mother and whose love and need for life was as great as any five-year-old child.

She changed during the month of August 1982. She became listless and quiet. She clung to her teacher's legs and refused to play at recess. She frequently complained of stomachaches. When asked why her stomach hurt, she said, "I think it's the soap I ate."

There were eighty-five possible witnesses subpoenaed for Donald McDougall's trial. Ursula told others she was afraid to go home because of Don. She told others she was not allowed to have water and was eating soap instead of food.

Ursula cried out in pain, in horror, and in helplessness…and no one heard.

We hear you Ursula. This is your story.

Part One

Ursula Sunshine:
A Child's Story

Chapter 1

Six Days of Torture

My name is Ursula Sunshine Assaid. I'm five years old. I'm a big girl now. My Mommy's name is Susan and she's from New Zealand. We live with Mommy's boyfriend, Don, in Altamonte Springs, Florida. My Daddy, Tom lives in California. He named me when I was born. He made my middle name Sunshine so my initials would be U.S.A. Mommy works at a restaurant in Orlando, Florida, so she is gone a lot. Don doesn't work much, and Mommy says I have to stay home with him. I'd like to tell you a story. It's about the last week of my life...

Monday

"I'm hungry," Ursula whimpered as she awoke. Startled by her own voice, the child cowered in bed. The little clock by her bed showed the hour hand at six.

I mustn't let them hear me. If they don't hear me they'll let me stay in bed. I don't want to go in the back yard again. I don't want to.

Ursula curled her frail body into a ball and tried to lose herself in the covers. Time passed without her being aware of it. Hunger gnawed in her stomach and would not allow her to sleep; sleep she so desperately needed for her abused body. Her mind made a desperate attempt to block out all conscious thought, in an effort to protect her from the nightmare that had become her life these past two months.

She felt the covers being pulled away.

"Mommy?"

She looked up, her large brown eyes filled with apprehension. Her voice was almost a whisper as she asked the slim woman standing over her, "Am I going to school, Mommy?"

"No," Susan Assaid replied, her voice was quiet, her mouth drawn in a stern line.

Ursula's fears confirmed, she begged in a whisper, "I don't want to go in the backyard again, please."

Susan turned away from her daughter, her face pinched with worry, marring her normally pretty features. She started rummaging through the dresser, pulling clothes out at random.

"You mind Don today. You hear me?" Susan turned her head toward her daughter long enough to see the small child nod in agreement. "I want you to be real good so he won't get mad. I don't want to lose him. He treats me real nice. Not like those others."

"Better than Daddy?" The child asked wide-eyed.

"Yeah, even better than your daddy." Her mother reflected. Ursula watched her mother move gracefully, but silently, around the room, her brown hair pulled up into a knot on top of her head.

I like it better when she wears her hair down, then she stays home with me.

Clothes were laid on the bed for Ursula and she slowly dressed herself in a blue T-shirt, pink shorts, white socks, and tennis shoes. She tried to put off the time that she would again have to stand under the tree in the backyard.

Ursula looked up at Susan, wishing her mother didn't have to leave and go to work. Maybe things would be different if she stayed home. Don had been nice to her before her mother had started working.

I'm so hungry.

Once again she took her post under the tree in the backyard. She had been standing by the tree for hours, every day, for more than a month. In the beginning she had toys and a plastic pool to play in, but Don had taken everything away. He had told her she was bad and that she had wet in the play pool, but she hadn't. Don didn't like her and said that she had lied. She thought he was the one who had lied.

2

The sun beat down on her even though the yard was shaded. There were at least four oak trees and one pine, but it didn't keep the Florida sun from reaching her. Her young body started to perspire and her blondish-brown hair became matted on her forehead. Flies buzzed around her. She fretfully slapped at the black pests, causing them to rise momentarily before they returned to attach again. Her mouth was dry and felt cottony because she was thirsty. All thoughts of hunger were forgotten.

She scuffed the toe of her shoe in the sand and watched the puffs of dust rise up and cover her white tennis shoes. Her eyes moved from one object to another: a tree, the leaves on the tree, a neighbor's yard, and the ants crawling past her feet. She counted them until she reached as high as she could go and then started over.

Her small body twisted and turned in discomfort. She had been made to stand until two or three o'clock in the morning the past few days in punishment for messing her pants. She hadn't meant to do it but he wouldn't let her in the house. When Don saw her clothes he made her sit on the toilet with her underpants over her head until long after her mother had come home.

I hate him, I hate him!

Her thoughts were the only form of rebellion she had as punishment was swift in coming if she opened her mouth to protest.

He's watching me. I can see the bedroom curtain move. He must have gotten up right after Mommy left. Why does he always watch me? Why won't he let me come in the house?

She watched the shade move across the yard as the sun changed its position in the sky. The day grew long and lonely. Her small, frail legs were tired and she was so hot. She heard the doorbell ring inside the house.

Could it be Mommy? Did she come back home?

3

Ursula summoned all the hope within her small body that her mother had come back and she would be freed from her prison under the tree. Her shoulders slumped in disappointment when she heard voices inside the house. It was only Don's friend. Don showed his friend where he was making Ursula stand. He moved the curtains just enough for the two of them to look out at her.

"I made Ursula stand up the whole weekend as punishment because she messed her pants," he bragged. "That's why she's not in school today. We couldn't get her up in time. Usually I make her go right to the tree and stand under it when she comes home from school. She needs to learn how to mind." Don looked at him expectantly.

"I guess so," his friend shrugged. "You never did tell me what the doctor said about her checkup."

"The kid's too small. She needs to eat more. He said to cut down on her liquids. He says she is small for her age, under four feet tall and her weight's down. She only weighs 30 pounds. So I cut out her liquids." Don shrugged as if it was a small matter.

Out under the tree Ursula continued to hear the mumble of voices. She couldn't make out everything they were saying but once in a while she could hear Don tell his friend about her.

He was mad at me again last night. I tried to be good after he let me get off the toilet. I didn't lie! I didn't! I couldn't help it if I swallowed some water when I brushed my teeth. I didn't do it on purpose. Why doesn't he like me anymore? What did I do? I want to be good. I don't lie. I don't!

The curtains in the front room moved suddenly. Two fingers gripped the side of the fabric and a thin sharp face peered through the opening. Ursula watched. She held herself still until the fingers released the fabric and she was once more alone in the backyard without Don's eyes peering at her.

Her legs trembled yet she knew she didn't dare sit down. Sitting down would make him angry and she tried not to think

4

what would happen if he became angry. She felt the urge to go to the bathroom. She crossed her legs, whimpering plaintively.

Oh please, please don't make me have to go potty.

The pressure became unbearable. Trying her best not to disgrace herself again, she knew only too well the outcome if she did. Minutes passed, minutes of agony as the pressure in her small bladder grew until she knew she couldn't stop it any longer. She held her small hand between her crossed legs but warm liquid still seeped between her fingers and dribbled down her legs. Her whimpering became loud enough to be heard. Ursula's small face turned white.

I'm bad, just like Mommy and Don said. I wet my pants. They told me not to wet my pants.

Slowly the tears welled up in her brown eyes and spilled down her face. She removed her hand from between her legs, bringing it up and staring at it before she wiped it on her shorts. She uncrossed her legs and squirmed at the uncomfortable feel of wet pants and legs and her shoes filled with her urine. She wiggled her toes within her shoes trying to relieve the squishy feeling. Staring at the house in desperation, she knew it was only a matter of time before Don ordered her inside. The tree became a refuge for her, the only safe place in her narrow world. She saw him peering out at her through a slip near the top of the front room curtains.

I want my Daddy. Why doesn't my Daddy come take me away? I'll be glad when Mommy comes home. I can't help it if I wet my pants. I'm so scared. I'm afraid. He always watches me from the window just before
...Mommy...please come home, Mommy ...I'm so scared.

"Ursula, get in here?" Don yelled.

Her body jerked as her little feet moved forward slowly. She tried to hurry, knowing she must obey him or risk adding to his anger. Sobs escaped her dry throat.

5

I've been bad. I know I've been bad. I'm sorry, I'm so
sorry.

"You wet your pants, didn't you?" he demanded as she entered the house.

"No", she answered, her voice more a plea of denial than defiance.

"You're a bad girl!" You know you wet your pants. Now you'll have to be punished." He yelled as he towered over her. His eyes were filled with a frightening gleam.

She watched as his tall wiry body moved toward the television. His large frame hid the screen as he reached for the brown belt on the top of the set. Her heart began pounding rapidly with fear as she saw his strong hand grip the leather strap and raise it over his head.

When she felt the sting of the belt on her buttocks, she jumped involuntarily. Again, the belt came down, causing pain to sear through her body. Again and again she felt the blow of the belt on her legs and buttocks. Her tears flowed freely as she pressed her hand to her mouth to muffle the sound of her crying.

"Get into the front room and stand in the corner? Keep your hands to your side. Don't move until I tell you. You little brat!" his voice echoed coldly throughout the room.

Ursula moved slowly. She held her little body in a rigid stance, her hands held stiffly by her side even while sobbing. Her shorts became a source of torture for her. The urine chafed her skin and her shoes continued to feel wet and squishy.

I wet my pants, big girls don't wet their pants. I'm
Sorry. I'm sorry. I'll be good.

She became aware of Don standing over her, a piece of soap in his hand, with his friend right behind him.

"Eat this, now! Bad girls must eat soap. You're bad, you lied," he sneered as his large hand moved nearer to her mouth.

Ursula's eyes were wide with fright. She hated the taste, but

6

she was too afraid to tell him. The hand in front of her shoved the soap into her mouth. A tangy, sour taste covered her tongue and the back of her throat. As she bit down, the sharp perfume scent shot to her nostrils and taste buds. She tried to force the soap down her dry throat but the white substance squeezed between her teeth and clung to her tongue, gagging her.

She watched him fearfully. Something in his face, an almost fanatical look of glee, kept her from spitting it out and asking for water. Long ago she learned not to ask for a drink because he would not give it to her. Finally, the awful substance was swallowed and lay heavily in her stomach.

Time seemed to stop as she was forced to stand at attention until her already-tired legs trembled and her feet burned in the wet shoes. Her stomach revolted as more and more soap was forced upon her. She ate until she could hold no more and then vomited. "Get your clothes off! You're a mess! You're a brat! Do you hear me? A spoiled brat!" Don turned and started pacing the floor. His face was tight with emotion. "I will make her mind. She will obey me. I will control her," he muttered as he paced. He looked at his friend. "She will learn to obey."

Ursula had been standing naked in the front room for hours when she heard her mother come home. Sometime in the hours she had been standing there, the friend had left.

Don left his place on the couch and went toward the bedroom. She could hear Don and her mother talking in the other room. She didn't dare turn her head to look, for she would feel the sting of the belt on her bare bottom. She cautiously shifted her feet and smelled the sharp ammonia odor of her urine. She still had not been allowed to wash herself after she had wet her pants.

The small hope she harbored that her punishment would end faded when her mother and Don came into the room and sat down on the couch. Don's voice bellowed out, "March, Ursula! While you're at it, I want to hear you say your ABC's. You better get them right, do you hear me, you little brat!"

Ursula looked to her mother for support but Susan showed no emotion. As usual, she remained at Don's side, not looking at

7

her daughter. Ursula lifted her tired feet and moved her aching legs, trying to do as she was told.

"A, B, C, D, E, F," she recited as she marched from the front room into the dining room; around each chair that Don had pulled out, thus providing a wider area to march around. "G, H, I, J," she continued, crawling under the café doors leading to the kitchen.

"Clean up the mess your brat made," Don ordered Susan as he pointed to the carpet. Susan quickly got up and went into the kitchen. She paused long enough to wipe Ursula off before returning to the front room. She stooped down and cleaned the vomit from the carpet. Looking at him fearfully, Susan quickly put away the rag and disinfectant. She did not pause in the front room but scurried on into the main bathroom. She grabbed several beach towels and covered the front room carpet, then docilely took her place beside him, a weak smile on her face.

Ursula entered the front room again.

"K, L", she paused, "N?" Don's strong hand curled into a fist and he swung at her. His fist buried itself into her small stomach, taking her breath away.

"You're wrong! Start over again and get it right this time." Don's face was twisted in anger.

Ursula tried to straighten up and do as she was told. She had been bad again. She had forgotten the rest of the alphabet.

I'm not supposed to make Don mad. Mommy likes Don better than the other boyfriends we've lived with. If I make Don mad he might leave and Mommy would cry. Why did I forget? Why am I bad?

"I'm sorry." Her voice came out in a low whisper from her aching chest. She tried again as she headed for the dining room; "A, B, C, D, E," she continued around the chairs and crawled under the café doors into the kitchen. "F, G, H, I, J, K, L," She faltered. "N?"

Don again clenched his strong hand into a fist and hurled it into her stomach. Her body curled itself around the fist as her head jerked back. Pain exploded in a red haze before her eyes.

Her stomach, already heavy with the soap she had been forced to eat, heaved up into her throat. Fear of being hit again made her swallow the sour vomit. She took small, gasping breaths until she could continue with her marching. She tried desperately to remember the rest of the letters.

"A, B, C, D, E." Her path took her again aground the dining room chairs and on into the kitchen. "F, G, H, I, J, K, L." She was sure this time. "M!" She didn't miss a step or mis-pronounce the letter.

The hours passed in a haze for Ursula. She was very tired. She continued to drag her feet around the rooms he had designated for her to march in. At some time during that hazy period she became aware of Don and her mother preparing their dinner and eating. They sat on the couch and ignored her as she marched by. Rarely did the two adults speak to each other. The only sound in the house was her voice reciting the alphabet and the low hum of the television set. Ursula had been forbidden to watch television weeks before that night.

Their dinner over, Don looked at Ursula. "Let's hear you count to twenty."

The brown leather belt lay near his hand on the couch. She was so tired now that she didn't absorb what he had said. She continued to recite the alphabet until the belt snaked out and struck her bare bottom. Her mother sat beside Don on the couch and watch silently.

"Not ABCs! Count, you little whore, count!"

Ursula flinched as the belt connected and her body burned. Tears welled up in her eyes and slowly ran down her face. She was too tired to make a sound other than what was demanded of her. Her throat burned from the many hours of reciting and from the effort to keep from crying aloud so she could continue to count. Repeatedly, her tired mind refused to come up with the next number in sequence and Don lashed out at her in punishment.

As she passed through the kitchen, her nose picked up the lingering aroma of their dinner and her stomach rumbled in protest. She had not eaten all day or had anything to drink. She

9

looked longingly at the faucet, wishing she could reach the tap and let the water pour down her parched throat.

I can't, I was bad, they told me so. I don't deserve anything to eat or drink, not a bad girl like me.

Ursula continued to march and count until late into the right. She no longer worried about her nudity. She was stumbling now. Don continued to beat her with the belt because she was unable to concentrate. Her words were slurred. Her body was trembling.

"Enough, Ursula. You are too dumb to say it right. I want you to stand right here in front of your mother. Don't you dare move. Keep your arms straight."

For a few precious moments there was blessed relief. Her body was too tired to hold her upright and she started to sway yet the fear of being hit again kept her from falling.

Hours passed. Don and Susan continued to lounge on the couch and watch television. Ursula stood with her back to the screen. Her small body, not yet giving up the fight, was held rigid against the treacherous weakening of her exhausted limbs. She knew punishment awaited if she allowed herself the relief of slumping to the floor.

"Let's go to bed, Susan," Don said as he moved toward the bedroom, pushing the child before him.

Ursula's legs were cramping as she slowly lifted each small foot. Somehow she made it into the bedroom, stopping short of stepping into the suitcase on the floor next to his side of the bed. "Go stand by my bed. Right there," he gestured.

"Stand inside that suitcase."

Ursula had severe stomach cramps from lack of food and the caustic soap Don had made her eat. Her tired eyes turned toward her mother. "Please, may I go potty?" she pleaded. All evening she had held back the urge to relieve herself but she could hold back no longer.

Her sight, blurred by fatigue, understood the movement of an adult head to mean approval and she moved as fast as her exhausted legs could carry her to the bathroom in the master

10

bedroom. She finished quickly before easing her small pain-filled body off the toilet seat. No longer questioning why she had to stand, she made her way over to the suitcase and tried to step inside. She stumbled when she was unable to lift her legs high enough to step over the raised edge. Don caught her by the arm and jerked her upright, calling her obscene names she was too tired to comprehend.

The lights were turned off and while Ursula could hear her mother and Don talking she did not try to make out what they were saying. What little energy she had left was directed at standing upright in the dark.

I'm tired, so tired. Sleep, I need to sleep.

She collapsed on his clothes in the suitcase. Constantly threatening Susan that he would leave, Don always kept his suitcase partially packed.

In the middle of the night, Ursula barely heard the shrill ring of the alarm clock. Her body had not moved a muscle as it tried to restore itself. Her escape into sleep was roughly halted when she felt his hands clamp around her arms as she was jerked from the suitcase. Her feet were slammed down on the floor.

"Stand up! I told you to stay standing! No one gave you permission to go to sleep!"

Ursula's body swayed as she attempted to make her legs stay straight under her. Her muscles cried out for rest yet her mind had awakened to the danger of disobeying him. Though she swayed from fatigue Ursula did not let herself fall asleep. Meanwhile, Don went back to bed.

Ursula continued to stand until once again she collapsed. As the gray light of dawn shone through the bedroom window, Susan awoke enough to check on Ursula. Unable to see her child's form in the darkness, she assumed Ursula was asleep on the floor by Don's side of the bed. Carefully, she made sure he was asleep. She then could allow Ursula to continue to sleep. She carefully lay back and nestled down under the covers.

Tuesday

Susan woke up quietly. She quickly, fearfully, checked to see if Don was still asleep. Raising herself up a little further, Susan looked over where Ursula had been standing. Not seeing her, she eased herself out of bed, tugging gently on her nightgown to loosen it from under Don's leg so as not to awaken him. She went over, gathered her child up in her arms and shook her gently.

Ursula's small, frail body fought being awakened. She tried to curl up in a ball and protect herself. She groaned and felt a hand clamp down over her mouth. Fear shot through her. Sleep was dashed from her brown eyes as she opened them wide and her body stiffened.

Mommy?

Her eyes pleaded with her mother to let her go back to sleep. She didn't have the strength to stand outside under the tree.

Ursula felt herself being placed upright in the suitcase. Her mother silently cautioned her not to make a sound as she pointed to Don and then left the room. Ursula could hear water running in the adjoining bathroom. The very sound brought back in full force her own desperate need for water.

A whimper escaped from her throat before she could stop it. Again her eyes widened in fear. Ursula looked at Don and prayed that he would not wake up. She clasped a hand over her own mouth as her mother had done, and tried not to cry. She dared not leave the suitcase. She could not call out to her mother for a drink of water. Either action could awaken him and her nightmare would start again.

Ursula again listened to the sounds coming from the bathroom. She could hear her mother brushing her teeth, taking a shower, and opening and closing the medicine cabinet. Each time she heard water being turned on, or shut off, her thirst would overwhelm her.

12

Susan returned to the bedroom dressed for work. Ursula knew she would again be left alone all day with Don.

Would Mommy leave me if I was a good girl? Why can't I be good? I don't mean to swallow water when I brush my teeth or go potty in my pants. I don't mean to. Oh Mommy, I'm sorry. I try to be good.

Fear kept her from uttering one word, but her eyes followed her mother as she left the room. Once again she listened to the sounds Susan was making, trying to identify them in an effort to keep her mind off her tired body and the increasing thirst growing in her throat.

She heard dishes clattering and water running. Even the sound of an egg sizzling in a pan came to the young child's attuned ears.

Don awoke and looked over at Ursula and then at Susan as she reentered the room.

"Did you stand all night?" he asked her.

Can I lie? If I don't it means more punishment. I want to be good. I tried to do what I was told, but I'm too tired.

After a quick, pleading glance at her mother, she turned back to Don and said, "Yes."

Relief washed through her as he seemed to accept her answer. He got up and went into the bathroom. Again Ursula heard water running in the sink. Ursula tried to swallow but it was too painful because her throat and mouth were so dry. Too afraid to move, she continued to stand where her mother had placed her earlier. The heat of the day was already growing even though the air conditioner had been running all night.

"I got to go to work baby, we need the money," her mother answered her silent plea. "You be good for Don, you hear? Just do what he says and everything will be all right. I can't lose him, baby. I just can't."

Her mother turned away from her and left for work. She was alone with him. The nightmare had started again.

13

He directed her into the front room. She moved as fast as her tired legs would take her. If she could only stay out of his reach, she would be safe.

"I want to hear your ABCs. This time you had better do them right," Don told her.

Ursula tried to do as she was told, even though she had not been able to sleep long enough to restore her energy. She started marching again. Through the front room, to the dining room, around each dining room chair, crawling under the café doors and up on her feet again on through the kitchen. He followed her each step of the way. So far, she had gotten every letter right.

Don stayed in the kitchen while she continued on into the front room. She could hear him cooking his breakfast. The overpowering aroma of bacon and eggs frying caused hunger to rise up sharply within her. Her legs, weakened from lack of food, water and rest, threatened to buckle under her. She straightened herself up and continued on. Her throat was sore from lack of water and overuse the day before.

She continued to recite, afraid to stop for even a second. Entering the dining room she stumbled when she saw Don. Fear shot through her and made her quickly pick up her faltering feet as she marched around each dining room chair. He was sitting, eating his breakfast, seemingly oblivious to her. She continued marching into the kitchen. Her body slumped in relief at being out of his sight.

Time and time again, she marched through the house, reciting her alphabet. Never able to stop and rest. Never given anything to eat of drink.

She grew more and more nervous of him as she marched by. He had moved to his usual place on the couch. His eyes watching, always watching as if he was waiting, hoping she would make a mistake. Tiring quickly because of her lack of rest and the unnerving look in his eyes, she stumbled over the alphabet.

His large hand, clenched up in a tight fist, struck her stomach. Her small body curled up over his large fist as the blow landed. The air left her lungs and a blackness descended over her eyes.

14

Unconsciousness was not to be. Terrified of another blow, Ursula tried to straighten up. Unable to do so quickly enough, she moved away with her body still bent and tried breathlessly to start reciting again. He got up from the couch and she feared he would hit her again. She watched him warily as he left the room. Her fear heightened when she saw him return with soap in his hand.

"I told you, you'll learn to mind me. You're nothing but a brat. You're always in the way. If you can't do as you're told, you deserve to be punished," he snarled at her.

She gagged as he shoved the soap into her mouth. Her throat closed up and she could not swallow. She tried again, her eyes watching him, afraid of his reaction to her gagging. From some blessed source, a small amount of saliva entered her mouth, enabling her to choke down the only piece of the soap.

Her stomach, already churning from the caustic action of the soap she had been fed the day before, rejected the piece she had just swallowed. Vomit rose up in her throat, and poured out of her mouth, earning her yet another blow to her stomach and yet another piece of soap to eat. Her bare flesh shivered with chills.

Holding the second piece in her mouth until her stomach stopped churning, she gagged again on the overpowering taste of perfume and sulfate. Afraid to spit it out she attempted to swallow, finding it took several tries before she could finally swallow all of it.

"Ursula, march!" he instructed from his usual position on the couch, his eyes blazing.

Her young legs made a valiant attempt to do as she was told. Unsteadily, she started her route through the front room, into the dining room, around each chair, and on into the kitchen. Long before she reached the front room, she knew she had again mixed up the order of the alphabet. Stoically, she advanced into the front room and received her punishment for being "bad." As the large fist buried itself in her stomach and she lost her breath again, her mind went blank.

Sometime during the day, Don's friend had come over again. The sound of their voices brought her back to an awareness of her surroundings.

"Ursula!" Don stopped her marching when she passed him and his friend as they sat on the couch. "Did you leave this candy wrapper on the table?" He asked as he pointed to the offending item.

"No."

"Who did?" Don asked slyly.

"Jenny did, I didn't."

"You lie!" Don shouted. He reached over and slapped the little girl in the mouth and then turned to his friend. "I'm probing her mind to help her work it out. I'm going to reprogram her until she learns to obey me; I will break her stubbornness."

"March, you little whore, march!"

She marched and continued reciting and standing through out the day, removed from her conscious self almost as if she was standing outside of her own body and watching herself be punished.

Jenny, I must find Jenny. Jenny will love me. She won't hit me. Jenny, come play with me. You don't mind if I'm in the way, do you? You're always there when I need you. You even let me put the blame on you for something I do wrong. He beat Kimmy too. Did you know that Jenny? I heard him tell Mommy. Kimmy is his little girl because he married her mommy. I'm not his little girl, but he beats me. He doesn't want me around 'cause I hear things. He's afraid I'll talk and the police will find out he steals things. But I won't talk. Honest I wouldn't Jenny, 'cause then they would take him away and make Mommy sad.

Ursula continued to think about her make-believe friend, closing out all sounds and feelings outside herself. Even the slam of the back door did not arouse her as Don and his friend went outside. Gradually she became aware of the thud of a basketball hitting the side of the house. Don was there. He hadn't gone far. She had to be good.

Jenny, Jenny, talk to me. I'm scared, Jenny. He won't leave me alone.

16

Ursula found comfort in her make-believe friend, retreating from her world of hurt once more.

All of a sudden she focused on the fact that her mother had come back. There was no sound of the basketball hitting the wall. Don had left. She slumped to the floor in relief.

"Ursula, didn't Don tell you to stand?" Her mother admonished her as she came into the room. Susan reached down, grabbed her, and pushed her up against the wall. Fear grew in Susan. She had seen Don peering in at Ursula when she had come home from work. He could come in at any moment.

I'm tired, Mommy. I don't want to stand. Please don't make me stand.

"Shh! Don't talk!" Susan warned Ursula. "You know Don doesn't want you to talk. Stand up and be good until he comes back. Maybe you won't have to stand anymore. If you're good, maybe he will let you play with your toys."

Ursula looked up at her mother but her legs felt very tired. She slumped back down to the floor. The enticement of playing with her toys no longer interested her. Susan forced tears to her eyes in an effort to get Ursula to obey her before Don returned.

Ursula's heart swelled with pain and tears filled her eyes. "Don't cry, Mommy. I love you. I'll be good. Don't cry."

Don often stood outside the window to make sure Ursula or her mother had not disobeyed him. If he heard Ursula talking he would storm back in and yell at her and then leave again to take his spot outside the window.

Ursula remained standing even after her mother left her to go to the phone.

"Don is making Ursula stand again." Susan told her friend over the phone. "She's been standing for several hours. He won't give her any food or water. I don't know what to do. When she collapses he makes her stand up again."
Her friend told her, "Take Ursula and get out of there!"

Susan shook her head in denial. "I can't, I can't leave him. I gotta go. He's coming back." She quickly hung up and moved

17

over to the couch. She sat quietly, with her hands in her lap, not focusing on anything.

Mommy is not going to give me any water or take me to the store like she used to, because Don is back and he is telling Mommy how bad I've been. Mommy always does what he wants. She's changed since she met him. She doesn't talk to me the way she used to. She let him hurt me, but I was a bad girl. I should be punished. They told me so.

"She's a spoiled brat!" Don shouted at Susan. "She deserves to be punished. You know she lies. She wets her pants. She will not mind. She needs to be controlled. It's up to you to make her mind. You must do as I tell you."

"She can't have been that bad, Don." Susan pleaded with him. Her face was pinched and white as she struggled within herself. "Must I?"

His sharp features stared back at her, showing no mercy in his desire to dominate. He nodded his head slowly and pointed to the soap in the bathroom, forcing Susan to bring it into the living room.

Susan stood in front of Ursula, holding out a piece of that soap. She looked up at her mother, her eyes pleading.

I don't want to!

Her eyes said what her lips could not. Fear held her tongue. The soap was pushed into her mouth. She clamped it shut and tried once more to chew the soft, squishy substance.

Again her stomach rejected it and the sour vomit came back into her mouth. Horror spread through her as she realized that not only had she vomited again, but she couldn't stop diarrhea from running down her leg onto the beach towel beneath her feet.

"I told you! I told you she was no good. You don't know how to raise her. Look at your kid! She's a mess," Don screamed, his face contorted with hate. Susan backed away from him in fear.

18

Punishment was swift in coming to Ursula. Even though she felt shame and anguish he still beat her. A whimper escaped her open, gasping mouth. The standing had come to an end.

"March, you little whore!"

I can't stop. I must not. It will mean more pain. More punishment. I have to keep going. Please don't let me fall down.

Somehow she found the strength to push her almost numb, wobbly legs forward and tried to hold back the tears.

Even though she tried to ignore the sounds of a faucet running, Ursula could not completely block out from her mind her need for food and water. Involuntarily, her eyes sought out the source of the sound. Her mother was standing at the sink washing her hands, ridding herself of the last traces of soap she had just fed her daughter.

The sun had gone down but Ursula had not been aware of it. The air conditioner continued to blast out cold air. The heat of the afternoon no longer beat down on the house with such ferocious intensity. Her body began to feel the chill. Not even the continued marching could keep her warm. Her small abused body was feathered with chill bumps and she was shivering.

Don and Susan were in the kitchen. Ursula watched them as she marched through but they did not bother to acknowledge her. Her frail body relaxed, just the slightest bit as she managed to pass by them without receiving punishment. Her small legs carried her from the kitchen, to the front room, to the dining room, and around each dining room chair.

Once again, her body tensed as she neared the kitchen. She jerked as she heard the back door slam shut. Hope flared up in her after Don left.

She continued to recite. Her mother was preparing dinner. Hope remained with Ursula until she marched through the kitchen and into the hallway. Her mother never once looked at her. Her body hunched in defeat. Her mother wasn't going to rescue her or let her rest.

19

Time once again became a blur as the aroma of meat frying and the sound of a pot boiling reached Ursula. Her stomach clenched when no food was forthcoming. It was one more thing she had to endure, one more thing that seemed to go on and on.

Don was back. Both he and her mother were sitting on the couch. Still she marched through each room, slowly now, so very slowly. Her little feet dragged her tired body from room to room. He hadn't hit her for a while. It had been long enough so she could almost forget what it felt like as the need for food and water overtook her fear of being hit.

Pointing to a place to one side of him, Don told Ursula, "Stand over here."

She stood, her arms stiff at her sides, trying not to look at Don and her mother. They were eating their dinner and watching television.

Maybe I' m not really here. Maybe if I am quiet they will forget me. That's why they don't feed me. I only think I'm real. I'm not real at all. I hurt. If I'm not real, why do I hurt?

"Here, you make her mind. Hit her until she continues to march and say her alphabet right." He was holding the belt out to her mother.

They haven't forgotten me. Did Don tell me to march? I didn't hear him.

Susan took the belt and looked first at Ursula, then at Don, indecision written clearly on her face.

"Go on, punish her," he told Susan.

Her hand flicked forward. The belt bit into Ursula's bare flesh. A burning, stinging pain radiated from her buttocks up her back. She cried out in distress. The belt landed again and again. Her bottom and the backs of her legs quickly turned beet red. Sobs shook her young body. The pain intensified as the belt connected time and time again, until Ursula could take no more and fell in a heap on the floor.

Susan grabbed Ursula's arm and jerked her upright.

The belt found its mark, lashing around her bare bottom. Her sobs became louder as the belt struck her bare skin. Over and over again until, a second time, she collapsed on the floor.

Susan took the perfumed sap on a rope Don gave her, reached down and again jerked her child upright, then placed the rope around Ursula's neck and shoved the whole bar into the child's mouth.

"Eat!"

Ursula spit out the foul-tasting substance. She could no longer submit to the cruel punishment. The belt hit her again and the child collapsed. Once again, Susan jerked her upright and shoved the soap into her mouth.

"Eat!"

Susan struck her four more times as she continued to hold on to the child's arm. Susan then put the belt beside her on the couch.

"March," she ordered her daughter. Susan jerked her forward and pointed to the soap. The child no longer rebelled but did as she was told. She picked up the soap and took a bite from it, gagging as she did so. The remaining bar fell away to hang from her neck. She chewed slowly, sobbing and marching as she chewed.

Don shoved the remaining soap back into her mouth as she marched by. The overpowering taste caused her to instinctively spit it out. He grabbed Ursula by the arm, took the soap and rubbed it in her face. She closed her eyes and screwed up her mouth to protect herself from the stinging substance. He took her small chin between his thumb and forefinger, yanked her mouth open, then shoved the soap inside.

"March!" the order was given. She marched, the soap gagging her until she was given permission to let it drop from her mouth and start counting.

"1...," a sob was torn from her, "2, 3," she could not suppress a cry, "4,5." She marched from the front room into the dining room.

I'm tired, so tired. Mommy, I hurt.

21

Each word was brought forth from the very depths of her soul, but so quietly that no one heard her. She had learned not to complain aloud.

"How long must she march?" Susan asked Don timidly.

"I don't know," he answered without turning his attention from the television.

Once again the child came into their line of vision. He reached out and stopped her marching. Grabbing the soap, he shoved it back into her mouth.

"Eat, all of it!"

She stood before them, trying her best to do as she was told. The highly perfumed substance would not go down. She gagged, vomited and gagged again. He shoved the soap back into her mouth even as she vomited again and ordered, "Eat, all of it. March, you little whore!"

Hours passed slowly while Don and Susan lounged in the front room watching television. Ursula continued marching until he motioned to her mother that it was time to go to bed.

She was to receive no rest that night. Once more, her naked body was made to stand in the suitcase beside their bed. He would make sure she stayed standing throughout the night by setting the alarm.

Wednesday

Ursula felt herself being shaken awake. Her body and mind cried out for the healing sleep she so desperately needed. Susan did not have to put her hand over Ursula's mouth this morning. Not a sound, not even a whimper, came from the young child. Slowly, she opened her big, brown eyes and focused on Susan. Once again her mother was going to work and would leave her alone with Don.

She stood in the suitcase at her mother's urging. Her body was numb. She closed her eyes and slept. Covers rustled on the bed beside her.

Wake up! Wake up!

Her mind alerted her to danger. Don was waking and he must not catch her asleep even though she had remained standing.

"How come this kid isn't out in the back yard? This is the second time it has happened. Didn't I tell you to put her out there before I woke up?" Don demanded of Susan.

"She's going," Susan whined as she grabbed up the child and took her out of the room. It didn't take long before she had her dressed and out in the yard.

Ursula stood under the oak tree. Her sad eyes gazed across to the empty yard next door. She turned her head and looked over into the park on the opposite side. Don played basketball and softball over there. If he wasn't in the house watching her, he was watching her from the park.

Her small shoulders slumped. She was so tired and hungry. It was an aching fatigue from days and weeks of standing and marching. It was a fatigue that had seeped into her very bones and while she had cried and pleaded for rest, none was given to her. Her dark blonde head drooped down and her eyes saw only the ground below her.

Hours passed. The sun had peaked in the sky and started its descent. During that time Ursula had heard her mother leave for work and the hum of the television set as Don stayed in the house. For once she felt no need to go to the bathroom because she had not had anything to eat or drink for several days.

It was torture for her to stand hour after hour. Sounds came from the park, happy sounds: children playing, lawns being mowed, men working. People stopped and stared at her from time to time before shrugging their shoulders and moving on. A neighbor entered her backyard and started to hang out clothes. She too stopped and looked toward the tired child. She shook her head at what she saw and continued on with her work. Not once did she turn back to look at the lonely child. Ursula was too tired to call out for help even if it would have been given. She no longer believed or even thought about kindness in others. They had things to do and places to go in their world. It was a world removed from her own.

The sun filtered down on her through the oak leaves. Two more oaks and a pine tree, with its pungent smell, stood tall in

23

the yard. For her the shade was not enough as the hours passed and the heat intensified. Her thirst and hunger were consuming her.

Ursula raised her head slowly and gazed at the back of the house. The windows glared back at her as if they also forbid her from being inside. Sometimes she would see a curtain move as Don looked out and checked on her. She could feel his waiting: waiting for her to shame herself and waiting for some reason to start the punishment again. She tried so hard to stand straight and still. She wasn't successful. Her legs trembled and jerked. Her head drooped and she closed her eyes. The heat added to her sleepiness.

It became too much and she could stand no longer. Her legs gave out and she slumped to the ground.

I have to stand. I must get up.

Slowly, she pushed herself up with unsteady arms but she still faltered. Her tired legs did not want to hold her. Her young arms pushed her up from the ground. Finally her twitching legs held her upright only moments before the curtain was pulled back and his eyes peered out at her. A car drove up in the driveway.

Could that be Mommy? Will they bring me inside now? Oh, no!

The pressure was growing in her bladder building until it hurt. She tried hard to be good. Her thin legs were crossed in a last effort to keep from doing what she had been told she should not do.

A car door slammed, the motor revved up, and the car drove away. She heard steps on the sidewalk. The front door shut. Ursula waited.

Where is Mommy? Why doesn't she come outside?

She could hear people in the park laughing and playing games. School must be out because more children were there. Some came and stood silently on the other side of the fence. They stared for a time before running back to their play. They had been forbidden to talk with her. It didn't matter because fear kept her from calling out to them.

The warm liquid she had been holding in until it hurt, ran down her legs. Again she had dis obeyed her mother and Don. She was bad.

"Ursula, get in here!" she heard Don yell.

She walked slowly to the back door. Her head hung down and she could see the path where the urine had run down her dirt-incrusted legs.

Inside the house, she entered the front room and stood in front of him. For once he wasn't looking at her but at her mother.

"She's a brat! She's the worst kid I've ever met," Don told Susan. "Kimmy was a good girl, she did what she was told."

Kimmy was the daughter of Don's wife. Don's wife had left him and was divorcing him, with the divorce to be final in a few days. Ursula had heard him tell her mother about it.

"I can solve the whole problem of Ursula obeying." He threatened, "I'll take her up on the roof and throw her off. She won't disobey me anymore."

"If you did that, it would kill her." Susan said, horrified.

"It would solve the problem."

Does Don want to kill me?

"Did you wet your pants?" he asked as he turned his attention to the small girl standing near him. She looked up and her body trembled with fear.

"No," she shook her head as she bit down on her lip, "Jenny did it."

"You lie! You're a bad girl! You're a brat! Go take your clothes off," he said as he pointed to the bathroom.

She went, although not willingly. She wanted to take her wet pants off but hated having to stand naked in front of Don and her mother.

25

As she reentered the front room he looked at her and said, "March!"

Her legs, already weary from standing most of the day under the tree, threatened to buckle under her. Still, she made them obey her will and started marching while looking over her shoulder.

Does he really mean to throw me off the roof?

She made sure she had the alphabet right. She did not want to give him any more reason to hurt her.

She marched into the kitchen, the hardest room for her to go through. Here she could see the water faucet. Her thirst increased every time she marched through that room. Her empty stomach rumbled as she passed the refrigerator. Hunger overwhelmed her and made her stumble over her letters.

Don stopped her as she came into the front room with a piece of soap in his hand.

"You lied to me."

Her eyes filled with fright but she opened her mouth automatically, took in the repulsive soap, and tried to swallow it. Nothing could stop her from gagging, unable to swallow, because of the lack of water, the soap stuck in her throat. She swallowed again and again hoping to dislodge it. Finally, with tears in her eyes, she swallowed it. She started marching again.

Faithfully reciting the alphabet, she went into the dining room and crawled under the café doors. Each letter became harder to say as her throat, coated with soap, almost refused to give up the words. She passed through the kitchen while reciting perfectly.

This time he had the belt. She made it back into the front room before making a mistake. She felt the sting on her bare flesh. The burning sensation went on much longer because her small buttocks were deeply bruised. Hoping to evade another lash of his belt, she moved a little quicker.

"A, B, C, D, E." She was out of the front room and back into the dining room. Her tired legs carried her around each dining room chair. She couldn't keep her eyes from straying to the

26

faucet as she entered the kitchen, but it seemed they had a will of their own. How she yearned for a drink.

Don ordered her to count hoping to force her to make a mistake. Ursula lost track of the sequence of the numbers. His belt stung her flesh again and again. He started yelling obscene names at her but it no longer had the same impact. She tried not to whimper between saying each number but she often failed.

"Stand in front of the couch. Right there," he pointed to a spot near him. She moved to obey. She had been standing or marching for over nine hours. It was now five o' clock.

Susan begged Don, "When is this going to stop? She needs rest. She needs to sleep."

"When she learns to obey me."

"She needs to go back to school. They will start questioning her absence. When is this going to stop?" Susan pleaded with him.

"Six o'clock tonight," Don answered curtly.

Water running again. She licked her dry lips and turned her head ever so slightly toward the kitchen. Her mother was fixing dinner. She could tell because of the sounds and aromas coming from the kitchen. Ursula looked at Don.

Will he let me eat tonight? He isn't watching me. His eyes are on the television.

She turned back and stared with blurred eyes at the wall over the couch. Her shoulders were slumped, her knees bent, and even her head drooped. She was so tired. So very tired.

"Ursula, tell me about Jenny."

"Jenny is my friend." The child's words were slurred from exhaustion.

"If Jenny is your friend, why does she get you in trouble?"

"Jenny doesn't. Jenny loves me."

"Jenny made you wet your pants. Jenny lied, didn't she?"

"Yes, but Jenny is my friend."

"Tell Jenny she has to obey me, Ursula. Tell Jenny…."

"What are you trying to do, Don?" Susan asked tentatively, from the kitchen door.

27

"Probing her mind. I will be obeyed."

Susan grimaced, "Don, you know Jenny is just a make-believe child."

"I'm going to help her work it out. I will reach her subconscious. She will obey me."

The questions went on and on. Ursula tried to answer but a gray fog clouded her mind.

Susan came in some time later with two plates of food. Ursula continued to stand and stare at the wall while her mother and Don ate.

Dinner was over and he looked at his watch and got up. He motioned for Ursula to come with him. They both went into the bedroom.

"Stand there." He ordered, pointing to the suitcase. She moved over to the side of the bed and lifted her sore feet, one at a time, into the case. Don then undressed in front of Ursula and got ready to go to a softball game. He opened the closet door and moved everything on the shelf to one side. She cringed when he came near her.

What is he going to do? Is he going to throw me off the roof now?

Her little body tensed when Don grabbed her, walked over to the closet and lifted her up on the shelf. The shelf was hard but it was still a relief not to stand any longer. It was a short-lived relief as she watched him shut the closet door.

It was dark and she was alone. What relief her body might have felt because she wasn't standing was lost as she stiffened.

I'm afraid. Mommy, I'm afraid.

When she was younger her mother put her in her room, turned off the light, and shut the door. Ursula would pound on the door and cry because she feared the dark room. Her mother didn't come back to let her out.

She had been sobbing in the dark closet for half an hour when her mother opened the door. Susan took her down and went into the bathroom. She bathed her small daughter and put her to bed. The bed felt so soft and welcoming to the child. Here was safety. Here was rest. She closed her eyes and slept.

Hours later Don reentered the house. The smell of beer was overpowering. "We won! The guys and I celebrated by pouring beer over each other." For once he was in a good mood and showed affection toward Susan.

Thursday

"I'm awake, Mommy," Ursula told her mother sleepily as she rubbed her eyes. Although she had slept for twelve hours, she was still tired and very thirsty.

"You're going to school today. Get up and get dressed. Be quiet. Don is still sleeping."

Ursula was as quiet as possible when she dressed. She didn't want him to wake up. Her mother brushed her hair and took her to the front door.

"Here is a note for your teacher. You are not to drink any water at school. Do you hear me? This note tells your teacher not to let you have any water. Don't you talk to the other kids either. You know what will happen if you do and Don finds out."

The young child could only nod her head as a shiver went down her back at the thought of any more punishment from him.

She went out the front door and moved slowly toward the bus stop. The other children were laughing and playing. She was too tired to do either. The kids were already used to Ursula not playing with them. They had been told she wasn't allowed to talk to them because she had misbehaved. They were now used to her quiet manner and separation from them, unlike the bubbly, outgoing little girl they had known just a few short months before. She stood silently watching the other children with sad eyes. They had been her friends until her mother told her she couldn't play with them anymore.

"Ursula how are you doing?" A neighbor asked as she approached the bus stop with her children. "We haven't seen you for a while. Are you all right?"

"My stomach hurts," Ursula answered the neighbor. She liked the lady. She had allowed her to play with her children before Susan had stopped her.

"Why does your stomach hurt, honey?"

"I don't know," Ursula hung her head. "I guess it's the soap I've been eating."

The neighbor appeared horrified. She shook her head sadly and then turned and walked back to her house as the children boarded the bus.

Ursula went listlessly toward her classroom, with the note from her mother in her hand. The teacher was standing by her desk. Ursula went up and placed the note on the desk. The teacher turned to her in surprise. "Why did your mother write that you couldn't drink water?"

"Mommy just said not to drink any."

"Thank you for bringing the note, Ursula. I'm glad to see you again." The teacher smiled down at her.

She has a nice smile.

Ursula was very careful that her dress covered any bruises that might show on the backs of her legs when she sat down at one of the round tables with three other children. She worried when people asked questions. She didn't want to get her mother in trouble or make her unhappy.

The day progressed slowly. She answered any questions asked her by the teacher. She did the work required of her but it took great effort. She was still very tired.

Recess came and she had to go outside. Ursula didn't want to play with the other children. She didn't feel like running and jumping. She stood by her teacher and clung to her legs. The teacher placed her hand on Ursula's head and smiled down at her as the child looked up.

She's nice. I'm safe with her.

No amount of coaxing by her teacher could get her to play. Finally, recess was over and she could go back inside and sit down. She could rest.

Will they notice that I don't have a lunch? What will my teacher say? My Mommy said I couldn't have lunch because I was bad. I'm so hungry. I want to eat. I'm thirsty, but I can't have any water.

She wanted water even more than lunch. Her stomach felt funny. Timidly she raised her hand and waited until her teacher responded to her.

"Please may I go potty?" she asked.

"Yes," the teacher replied, glancing at the clock. It was near lunchtime anyway.

Ursula waited a minute before leaving her seat. Afraid to wait any longer for fear her teacher would change her mind, she made her way quickly to the bathroom.

She slipped back into her seat just as her teacher called to all the children who were buying lunch to line up. The sound of chairs scraping and children giggling filled the room. She sat silently, her hands in her lap.

Her teacher left the room with those children who were buying their lunch. A teacher's aide called for all those who wanted to buy milk or juice. Just the sound of the words caused Ursula's mouth to water. The rest of the class proceeded to pull out their lunches from the cubby hole assigned them in the back of the room. Ursula went to her cubby hole. No lunch was waiting there, but she did not want anyone to notice. She kept her back to the class and clutched at her stomach with her small hands. The smell of sandwiches and fruit filled the air. The other children were talking and laughing as they ate.

I'm so hungry, but I was bad. That's why I can't eat because I was bad. I tried so hard to be good, but I always do something wrong.

31

The teacher's aide was unaware of one small girl sitting alone with no lunch. Most of the other children had finished eating by the time the teacher returned with her group. Class went on as usual.

School was over for the day and Ursula was trying hard to be a good girl like her mother wanted. She stood in front of the water fountain trying her best not to give in to the need to drink. Her mouth was parched. She could hardly swallow, so desperate was her need for water. The driving need to drink overcame her desire to please her mother.

She reached for the cool handle of the drinking fountain. Slowly she pressed it and watched the water spurt upward. Eagerly she pressed her mouth to the head of the fountain, drinking as much as she could. Quickly, she wiped her lips and cheeks and looked around to see if anyone was watching her.

The other children were running by her anxious to get to their bus. Time was running out. Ursula took one last drink. She ran toward the bus that would take her back home, back to her nightmare world.

The bus ground to a stop with a squeal of its air brakes. The double-doors swung open. Ursula rose slowly, gathered her belongings and moved with lagging feet to the front of the bus. The other children ran ahead with glee and laughter to their homes. She walked slowly knowing better than to go to the front door of the house. Instead she walked reluctantly toward the backyard. Suddenly she turned and ran to the house across the street. Tears welled up in her eyes and ran down her face.

I can't go back. I can't!

She banged on the neighbor's door with her little fist. Sobs wracked her body. "Please let me in. I don't want to go home. I want my mommy."

The neighbor cradled Ursula. She did not know what to do with the child. She was crying too hard to take her home and she wasn't sure it would be the right thing to do. It took her twenty minutes to calm Ursula down.

"You have to go home, Ursula. Honey, you can't stay here."

She took the child by the hand and reluctantly took her across the street. Ursula's sobs had calmed down until only an occasional shudder shook her small body.

The neighbor knocked on the door and then took an involuntary step backwards when Don answered. He was wearing a pair of white under shorts as he leaned against the door.

"Ursula has been at my place crying. She didn't want to come home."

"The kid doesn't like me. What can I say?" Don shrugged. He grabbed Ursula by the arm and pulled her into the house and closed the door. The neighbor left shaking her head.

"I told you to come right home, didn't I?" Don yelled at the frightened child, shaking her so hard her head snapped back. "Get outside where you belong. Don't you dare move."

Ursula went outside as quickly as she could. The day was hot and she was tired. She longed for sleep. Although she had slept the night before, it had not made up for the many other nights she had been forced to stand until she dropped from exhaustion.

She shifted her feet, trying to find a way to keep them from aching. They were sore from long days of marching and standing. Her big brown eyes looked up toward the house. She watched as the curtain moved slightly.

He's watching me again. I wish Mommy was home. If she was home, maybe I could come inside and be with her. If I'm very lucky, Mommy will take me to the store with her. I like to go to the store and look at all the different things. It's been a long time since Mommy took me there.

The sun beat down on her. The water she drank at school began to leave her body quickly. She started to sweat. Her legs grew weary. She had been watching the children play in the park next door until she looked toward the house. She tried not to look because she knew he was there.

I don't like Don.

33

While she watched, the curtains parted, and she saw eyes peering from the room.

That's not Don, it's my Mommy. Mommy is home. Why doesn't she come and get me?

She watched one set of eyes being replaced by another. Don was beside her mother. They were both watching her.

Do they know I've had a drink? Ohhh, I've been a bad girl. Why can't I be good? If I was good like I used to be then maybe I could play with the other kids again just like it was before Don got so mad at me. What did I do to make him hate me so?

She remembered her mother telling her, "You always get into trouble on Friday and screw up my weekends." Her mother was very angry when she said that. It wasn't even Friday yet and she had been bad again.

Is Mommy very mad at me?

The curtain fell back in place. Ursula continued to stand under the tree.

An hour passed. The need to go to the bathroom was growing. The fear of wetting her pants grew just as quickly. Heat flooded her body.

I can't wet my pants again. He'll hit me more.

She ground her teeth together in an effort to stop the pressure from building. When that didn't work, she clenched her hands and legs. Her whole body tensed as she reached down and pressed herself tightly with her small, thin hands. She quietly moaned. Her hands tried to stop the escaping liquid but it seeped through her fingers and down her legs. She had done it now. She had been bad again.

34

"Ursula, get in here,'" Don yelled at her from the bedroom window.

"Did you just wet your pants?" He asked when she entered the front room.

"Yes," she replied, her head still bent.

"Go get undressed."

She started to move toward her bedroom, her shoulders slumped, her head still bent until her chin touched her chest. Her tousled hair fell forward and over her small face. With one stride of his long legs he reached her. His strong hand clasped her shoulder. She flinched at his touch.

"That's not your room anymore!" He raised his hand and spanked her bottom hard enough to make her fall to the floor. "Take your clothes off right here," he demanded.

She looked up at his towering figure. Tears filled her brown eyes. Slowly she picked herself up off the floor and scurried into the front bathroom. She removed her clothes, feeling relief to be rid of her wet panties. Hesitating, she reentered the front room.

He pointed, his muscular arm extended full-length, "Get into the dining room. Go sit in the chair."

She passed him quickly and climbed up into a dining room chair. She watched as he went into the kitchen. The noise of a pan clanging against the stove caused her to jump. The sound and ensuring aroma of butter melting caused her stomach to rumble. She turned as her mother came into the dining room and stood by her chair. Susan took a long pull on her cigarette and blew smoke from her mouth. Her red lips were pulled tight as she looked down at her daughter.

"I told you that you always screw up my weekends. Why can't you be good?"

Ursula sadly turned her fear-filled eyes from her mother to Don as he entered the room. In his hand were two pieces of browned bread.

He made me a sandwich? Maybe he isn't so mad at me after all?

35

Her stomach clenched and continued to rumble in hunger. It had been a long time since she had eaten anything but soap. She watched as he came closer, the saliva forming in her mouth at the very thought of food.

"Eat," he ordered, as he thrust the sandwich at her. She took the bread from him and bit into it hungrily. The gritty, bitter taste of soap assaulted her taste buds. He had made her a soap sandwich.

I'm so hungry. Why did he make me a soap sandwich?
I'm sorry I wet my pants.

She turned her pleading eyes from his frowning face to Susan. She watched as her mother's eyes filled with tears. "I want you to stop; it isn't right." Susan pleaded with Don.

His thin, sharp face was stern as he retorted, "Of course it's right."

Ursula sensed the anger in the air. She became distressed, her heart aching at the sight of the tears in her mother's eyes.

I'm sorry. I was bad. I'll try and be good. Please,
Mommy, don't cry.

Hoping to make her mother happy, Ursula bit into the sandwich. No matter how hard she tried, she couldn't keep from gagging on the soap. Bite after bite she chewed, swallowed, gagged, and tried to swallow again. Finally the sandwich was eaten.

She put her hand to her mouth hoping to stop the vomit but couldn't.

"March!" he demanded, his body taut with fury.

She stood up and started her now-daily routine as her mother discarded her cigarette and rushed to clean up the vomit from the table. Don pulled back each dining room chair to give her a wider area to cover.

Time no longer had meaning to Ursula as she marched. She was already tired from a full day at school and standing under the tree. Her mind remained aware only enough to keep her

36

reciting her alphabet in the proper order. On and on she marched.

Ursula received another blow to her already-tender buttock. "Stand in a corner!" he ordered the small child. "You can't get anything right." He then turned, went to the telephone, and dialed a number.

Ursula turned back to watch him when she heard his voice raised in anger. She watched fearfully as his face grew red.

She could only hear his side of the conversation but it was enough to let the child know he was talking with his wife. His divorce would be final the next day and he didn't like that. Not one bit!

She faced the wall quickly when she saw him turn and look at her. She did not want that anger to be directed toward her.

Throughout the phone conversation, her mother had stayed on the couch and worked with her macrame. She would sneak glances at Don, and her mouth was drawn tight in anger until he was off the phone. She attempted to show disinterest.

It was nearing one in the morning. Don yelled at Ursula, "Go stand by my bed."

Her small, thin legs carried her tired body into the bedroom. She stopped at the side of the bed and slowly lifted her bruised feet into the case. She watched Don and her mother prepare for bed. The springs squeaked as they lay down. The light was shut off and the room became dark.

"I have to go potty," Ursula whispered into the darkness. She was afraid to ask but the pressure was unbearable. "Please," her small voice penetrated the darkness, "may I go potty?"

"Damn! Go sit on the toilet and stay there," Don told her. She went as quickly as she could in the darkness toward the bathroom. She made it to the toilet just in time.

He got up and positioned the bathroom door just enough to allow him a view of Ursula in the mirror. He got in bed and lay back to watch her, always watching her, until he grew drowsy. Then he settled down and went to sleep. She took advantage of the mirror to watch fearfully as the hours passed. She was afraid to move off the toilet seat. She was afraid.

Exhausted, she fought sleep until her head fell upon her chest and she slept.

Friday

Susan awoke and found Ursula asleep on the toilet. She clearly saw the bruises on her daughter's arms and legs.

Quietly, she got ready for work. She was putting on her makeup when her child awoke. Ursula looked anxiously at Susan, hoping her mother would lift her off the toilet. Susan put a finger to her lips to keep the child quiet.

"I like your outfit, Mommy," the young child whispered, hoping to please her mother. Susan looked down at Ursula then back into the mirror and smiled, but did not remove her from the toilet seat.

Don awoke and looked toward the bathroom. "Go make some coffee," he barked at Susan. She was quick to comply, leaving her make-up scattered over the counter in her rush. He got out of bed, his wiry body clothed only in under shorts, went into the bathroom and yanked the child off the toilet. "Go stand by my bed," he told Ursula.

Ursula had not been able to sleep except for small snatches of time during the night. She was exhausted. Her body was sore from sitting in such an uncomfortable position but she hobbled over to the suitcase and stepped inside. She jumped in fright when he slammed the bathroom door. She watched him dress and then he turned and came toward her.

What's he going to do?

Fear coursed through her body. "Follow me," he ordered. Her small naked body, chilled and tired, followed. He went into the kitchen, poured himself a cup of coffee, then turned and went into the dining room. She trailed him like a meek puppy afraid not to, yet uncertain what it was that he wanted her to do.

Where is Mommy?

38

Her hands were held stiffly at her side, in the same stance he usually demanded of her. She watched him drink his coffee, Hating him because he would not allow her even one small sip of water.

Susan came into the dining room and sat down with her coffee and a cigarette. "I don't want to go to work. Why don't I stay home and watch Ursula," she said tentatively.

"No! We both know we need the money. Since I was arrested, I have been unable to fence the rest of the merchandise."

Silence reigned while they both finished their coffee. Susan moved restlessly until she could not contain what was in her mind anymore.

"Don't hit her anymore."

"I won't."

"I think you're being overly strict"

"If I don't straighten her out now, she'll do something bad when she gets older. She'll listen to me. You should have done that to her a long time ago."

Susan looked regretfully at her young daughter and sighed. She got up from the table and gathered her belongings. She had to get to the bus stop if she was going to be on time for work. Susan left without looking back at the small naked body of her child.

Ursula, already chilled, shivered with fright. She was alone again with Don. She watched him with fear clearly visible in her eyes.

What's he gong to do to me today? I want to sleep. I'm hungry. Why won't they let me eat or drink?

It wasn't long before Don made his wishes clear. He went into the kitchen and sliced off pieces of gritty hand soap, returned to the dining room and put a piece into Ursula's mouth.

Periodically Don fed her the remaining pieces until he finished his coffee. He stood up, stretched, and motioned to her to follow him.

"Pick up your feet. Get moving. Start counting," he said lazily.

Ursula slowed her pace as she entered the kitchen and prolonged the time away from him, her hoarse voice calling out numbers. Again fearful, she looked toward him as she reentered the front room. She knew what was coming by the look on his face. He lashed out with the belt. The blow caught her on her legs. She jumped away and quickened her step as he yelled, "I told you to get moving!"

She tried to move faster but her exhaustion kept her from obeying. Each time she entered the front room he hit her harder. Her flesh rose up in red welts wherever the belt connected.

I hate him! I hate him! I want my Daddy.

Her legs, wobbly from exhaustion, slowed. Her feet dragged. Her voice croaked out the numbers as she passed him time and time again.

"Move it! Pick up those feet!"

"I have to go potty," she whimpered.

"March!"

She screamed back at him, "I got to go potty! I hate you! I hate you!" she no longer cared about punishment. The torture had gone on too long.

He grabbed her by her arm and swung her around to face him. He lifted his hand and slapped her across the mouth.

"I hate you!" She screamed defiantly. He drew back his hand and hit her again. Blood spurted from her lower lip. "I hate you! I got to go potty!"

Don jerked her up by her arm and carried her into the master bathroom; her feet kicking at the air as she tried to gain her release. He stood her on the toilet seat, her feet straddling the open hole.

Ursula wiped at her mouth and rubbed the tears from her eyes, leaving a bloody trail across her face. Her body emitted a greenish-while excrement that ran down her legs and into the toilet. She trembled as he turned and left the room.

Susan entered the front door. The sound of Ursula's screams filled the house.

I hate you! I hate you! I want to see my Daddy! I don't want to live with you anymore!

Susan rushed into the master bedroom. Afraid Don would stop her, Susan did not enter the bathroom but looked in the mirror on the bathroom door and saw Ursula standing on the toilet. She was horrified by what she saw and told Don, "She looks bad."

"Ignore her. She hates being ignored," he said as he waved his hand lazily at Susan.

Susan continued to look at Ursula. She noticed her swollen, bloody lower lip, blood on her face and fresh blood clots coming from her mouth. She also saw the excretion from her rectum while mucus flowed from her nose and tears from her eyes. Susan saw the bruises had darkened and there seemed to be more of them. She looked at Don. She started to say something but he cut her off. "Stay away from her. Ignore her. Don't even go near her!"

She looked first at Don and then at Ursula. She did nothing.

"March into the front room."

Ursula looked up at his towering figure and hatred filled her eyes. "Get down on your knees," he ordered Ursula. She hesitated for just a second, glanced at her mother, and then did as she was told. "Now, march. Don't get up. Stay on your knees. I want to hear the alphabet."

She remained on her knees, her body in an upright position, and started sliding forward. Her young voice rang out, "A, B, C, D, E, F, G."

She was scared as she watched him take a seat on a dining room chair by the door. Her mother remained on the couch, watching. Ursula felt he was waiting for her to make a mistake. She tried very hard to get through the alphabet without mixing up the letters.

It didn't seem to matter if she got the letters in the right order because Don lashed out at her with the belt every time she came

41

by.   Her already-bruised flesh felt the sting of the belt with greater intensity. Her knees soon became red and tender from the pressure and friction of her crawling.

Four hours passed before he allowed her to stand. It no longer mattered that her mother was also in the room sitting beside him on the couch, watching as he hit Ursula harder. Susan's eyes were watchful, her mouth taut yet she never uttered a word in her daughter's defense.

The emission of a greenish-white fluid from Ursula's rectum was almost constant now. He continually stopped her to shove another piece of soap at her and demanded that she eat it. Each time she forced it down as best as she could. Her act of defiance earlier had depleted her strength to show her hatred for her tormentor.

Don saw that hatred and it triggered a response from him. He got up off the couch and rushed toward her. He slapped her across the face with the back of his hand. His six-foot two frame loomed over her as she fell backward from the blow. The hatred in her eyes still grew even as she sucked air into her lungs and cried out loudly.

He straddled her with one knee on either side of her slight body. Fury was written in his face. He brought his fist up and struck her in the side, first with one fist and then the other. A terrified cry followed as each blow landed.

Don bent over the small child. He beat her with his fists, not caring where the blows fell. He would make her behave. She would obey him.

The blows landed on her head, her chest, and her stomach. Still the hatred was there for him to see. Her screams echoed in his ears.

"You little whore! You will learn to obey! Do you hear me? You no-good, little brat!" His words became more vile as he spat them at her, almost in rhythm with his flailing fists.

From a long distance away Ursula heard her mother scream. He didn't stop in his punishment of the child as he shouted out at Susan, "Go in the other room, if you don't like it. Never mind what is going on here."

42

Susan ran into the kitchen and held onto the counter top. "He's going to kill her if he doesn't stop," she whispered aloud.

"Get up, you little whore!" He yelled at the young child.

Susan pushed herself away from the counter and entered the dining room. She gasped when she saw her young daughter. Ursula's hands were held close to her chest and though she was standing upright, her legs kept buckling under her.

"You've hurt her permanently," Susan screamed at him. He glanced at her ominously before turning his attention back to the child.

Ursula's one thought was to get away from her tormentor. Her legs weren't working very well but she made them obey her command to move. Slowly she moved toward the master bedroom. She no longer worried about the emission from her rectum. It had been a constant part of her misery that she had long since ignored. Pain was intense throughout her body. Her frail legs barely managed to get her into the bedroom. She wanted to curl up on the bed and hug herself until the pain went away. Her bedroom was no longer hers—he had told her so—but she couldn't remember when.

He was right behind her and she could hear his heavy breathing from the effort it had taken to beat her.

"Go stand in front of the mirror. Look at yourself! Look and see how ugly you are." His face was contorted with emotion as he hovered over the child.

She stood in front of the mirror. Her refection showed a small, frail child whose skin was black and blue, her face, blood-streaked, hair in wild disarray, and her eyes wide with fear and hate. Her arms and hands were curled up on her chest and her legs buckled. Ursula didn't recognize the child in the mirror as herself. She felt sorry for that child.

She must hurt as much as I do. If Don and Mommy are here, looking in the mirror, then the child must be me. Do I look like that! I am ugly.

43

The child in front of her swayed. One look at Don's face kept her from giving in to the intense desire to sink to the floor. She remained standing.

"Go stand by the bed," he ordered. Ursula moved slowly with unsteady steps but she hurt too badly to continue to rebel, had she been aware enough to do so. Her mind and her world were slipping away from her.

Standing by the bed she heard the sounds of her mother and Don getting ready to go to sleep. The sheets rustled as the two got into the bed and turned off the light.

From deep within herself she found the strength and the will to remain standing as long as Don was awake. Her body kept swaying yet she remained standing. She stared at him and her eyes never left him. She waited. Her frail, abused body slumped down in sleep.

Saturday

Susan awoke. She carefully looked for her daughter. Only by leaning over could she see her curled up in a fetal position on her back. She would let her sleep. Ursula needed that sleep.

Susan was afraid. What if Don woke up and found Ursula sleeping? It would trigger mo re punishment. Her child couldn't take any more. The fear grew until Susan got up to stand beside her sleeping daughter. Gently she tried to pick her up. The child was almost a dead weight.

"Ursula you must wake up. You have to stand up before Don gets up. You don't want to make Don mad. Stand up," Susan whispered.

Ursula tried to stand but couldn't. Her eyes were barely open while her mother's voice slowly penetrated the haze of pain that gripped her body. At her mother's insistence she tried again to stand but her body would no longer obey her.

Susan needed to have Ursula stand. She couldn't let Don find her this way. Her poor child's face was puffy and her lower lip was swollen. Her nose was running profusely, but it was her

44

bloodshot eyes that scared Susan the most. She also saw Ursula's bruised legs and buttocks.

Don awoke and jumped out of bed. His face was livid with rage. Susan quickly backed away from her child. He grabbed Ursula around the shoulders and took her into the bathroom. He placed her on the counter and looked at her for a moment.

"Are you thirsty? He asked in a sly manner, with a mirthless grin.

"Yes," she whispered. She moved as though to reach out and plead with him. Her hand barely moved away from her chest before he hit her across the back of her head with his fist. Pain exploded in her head as she crashed to the floor.

"Ursula" Susan screamed, her face white with fear.

Ursula could hear the scream but it was far away. He lifted her off the cold , hard floor. His hands hurt her every where he touched her. Her head hurt tremendously. She tried to raise one crippled hand to soothe it but her arm would not reach that far.

She felt herself being lifted into the sink. Don left the bathroom. She looked toward her mother. Her sad eyes understood that her mother would do nothing to stop him. Susan stood near, but not touching her daughter. Fear and indecision were written on her face.

Don entered the room with container of ice in his hands. He slowly emptied the container on top of her. The cold struck her immediately and then with a burning ache it spread throughout her naked, bruised body.

He went out of the bathroom, his face expressionless. She followed him in the mirror with her eyes and watched as he lay back down on the bed and put his hands behind his head and went to sleep.

Susan stood for a moment looking at her daughter before she went into the bedroom. Ursula was left alone in the icy sink. Her body heat started to melt the ice but then was counteracted by the cold of the other ice cubes as they stuck to her skin.

It took a great effort to turn her head and look into the mirror on the bathroom door. She watched, her eyes out of focus, both Don and her mother. Ursula heard her mother crying.

45

The burning pain from the ice intensified as the hours passed. Ursula's head continued to ache and her eyes couldn't focus. In time, even the burning ache from the ice disappeared. Her body became numb, except for the racking pain in her head. Her body was bent over and she appeared to have no bones under her skin as she sat in the sink.

Susan stared up at the ceiling, thinking of her decision to put her lover before her daughter. Still she felt she could make no other decision. Don was the most important person in her life. She couldn't lose him.

Two hours later Don woke up and took Ursula out of the sink. Her skin was white and wrinkled because of the ice.

As he took her into the bedroom the jostling caused her head to throb with pain. Susan put a pillow behind her and eased her into a reclining position. He went into the bathroom, and returned and started to rub her legs with a heat inducing cream.

"Go make Ursula something to eat. This will make her feel better," he told Susan. She watched as her mother left the room. Her skin came alive to the burning sensation of the cream he rubbed first one leg then the other. He said nothing and his expression was cold and forbidding.

I hurt. Please be gentle.

He ignored her cries of pain. He continued to rub, his face devoid of any emotion. Finally he lifted her up and took her into the dining room and placed her on one of the dining room chairs. He pushed it toward the table until she was forced to sit up, only because she was wedged between the two. Her head slumped forward and she could not raise it to a normal position.

"Make sure she eats," Don told Susan and he sat down at the other end of the table. Anxiety appeared in his eyes. "Have I gone too far?" he murmured to himself.

Susan came into the room with a plate of scrambled eggs, a fork, and a spoon. She placed the items in front of her daughter and tried to give her the fork. Ursula's hands and arms were crunched up against her chest. She was unable to hold the fork in her hand and it dropped to the floor.

Susan took the spoon, scooped up some of the scrambled eggs and tried to feed her. With effort Ursula opened her mouth and accepted a small amount. Wanting to please her mother, she took in the food and held it within her mouth until she could find the strength to chew. Swallowing was very difficult because of the caustic reaction of the soap in her mouth and throat. After the second attempt to eat she shook her head and refused to try any more. Her hunger had left her.

Don looked at the child and then at her mother and said, "You'll have to nurse her back to being well. Put her back in the bedroom and then come back in here. She can lay down by herself." His fingers drummed nervously on the table.

Susan looked at him in defiance. She wanted to continue to feed her child. "There must be some way to make her eat. She hasn't had any food since Sunday night."

Don became impatient with Susan and scooped Ursula up in his arms. He carried her into the bedroom and put her down on the bed.

"I'm going out for a walk," he told Susan, agitation apparent in his voice.

"Where? For how long?" she pleaded.

"I don't know," he said in exasperation as he left the room.

I feel cold.

Susan touched Ursula's flesh. It felt cold and she was shivering. Susan placed a sheet over her, then put her hand on Ursula's forehead. Her skin became hot, but she still shivered with cold. Susan was frightened.

"Try to go to sleep," Susan said. She stayed on the bed with her daughter. Ursula's eyes remained open. The sleep she had craved for so long escaped her because of the pain that racked her body. She no longer felt cold but now her body felt on fire. Restlessly, the child kicked the covers off. She looked up at her mother, not really seeing her, and started to whisper.

Please be gentle. I've got to go potty.

Susan's hands were gentle as she lifted her daughter up, put her on the toilet carefully, and moved away. Ursula felt herself falling. She couldn't sit up. Her body was too weak to support her. Susan grabbed her and held onto her. A whitish fluid spurted out. Susan wiped her.

Be gentle.

Susan lifted her up and put her back on the bed. Don stalked into the room. He looked at Ursula with disgust. "Don't stay in here with her too long. Leave her by herself." The look on his face clearly stated he could no longer stand the sight of the child.

"I don't want to leave her by herself," Susan pleaded.

Don motioned for Susan to leave her anyway. She looked back at her daughter before she arose, reluctantly, and followed him from the room. His wishes still came first. "I think we should take her to the emergency room. She doesn't look good," Susan urged Don, giving him a haggard look.

"We can't! The hospital will know she was abused. They would turn us in. It would get us into trouble." Don was nervous and agitated. He got up and paced the floor, and ran his hands through his hair causing it to look even more disheveled than before. His sharp face tightened with anxiety.

Ursula stared into space, her body tormented with pain. Her nude body was both hot and racked with chills.

"Go to the store and get the kid some milk," Don told Susan. His worry of having gone too far this time continued to grow. Something had to be done to get her health back. "I don't want to kill the kid after all. Only make her mind," he told Susan. Susan left but not before she looked at him with accusing eyes.

Don stood over Ursula for a long while, just looking down at her, the coldness in his face amplified. She stared back at him. Her mind was whirling with the hate she felt for him, the only emotion she could now register in her battered mind.

48

The sound of a door opening and of pans being moved around in the kitchen came to her in a vague way. Her mother must have returned. The refrigerator door opened and closed. Don acted as though he did not hear anything. A cruel smile came to his lips as he raised his arm and pointed a finger at her. He used his hand as if it were a gun and said, "Pow! Pow!"

Her mother was in the room now and sat on the bed. Ursula's eyes followed her mother but she did not turn her head. Gently her mother lifted her head and replaced the pillows behind her. She tried to help her child drink the glass of milk she had poured. Don watched for a few minutes, snorted in derision, and stalked angrily from the room.

Ursula opened her tender, ulcerated mouth and sucked greedily at the first fluids she had received in two days. The cool, sweet taste flooded her senses and although she was exhausted she drank as much as she could.

Don came back into the room. Ursula's eyes followed him.

"Leave her alone! She's not a baby. If she wants to drink, she can drink it herself." Don went to the bedroom door then turned and looked at Susan, "Leave...her...be!"

Ursula's eyes turned back to her mother. Gratitude shone out of them for the milk her mother continued to hold up for her to drink, and again when her mother wiped off her body secretions. That gratitude slowly diminished when her mother eased her back onto the pillow and left her alone in the large bed after putting a sheet over her. She then was alone for hours with her pain and the loss of fluids from her small body. Her mother had once again chosen Don over her.

The shadows in the room lengthened. She could feel the need to go to the bathroom again. She again could not stop herself because she no longer had control over her body.

"Can I go into the other bedroom?" She asked her mother the next time she came into the room. "I want to look at the plants. I don't like it here."

"Don doesn't want you in the other bedroom," Susan answered as she lifted her daughter up and took her back into the bathroom. Ursula was unable to hold herself up, her body slumped forward, and her head almost touched her knees.

Susan soon picked her up and eased her back on the bed and cleaned up the area around her. She covered her child with a sheet once more before leaving her alone again.

Susan came into the room frequently and took her to the bathroom. Each time a spurt of whitish liquid would spew forth. The discomfort it brought did not penetrate the child's mind. Even her nose and eyes had begun to run with a yellow mucus but this too was only a small part of her hazy world of pain. Susan tried to give her child a drink of water but Ursula found it hard to swallow. Ursula remained in the fetal position with her arms tucked up against her chest and her legs drawn up. Her skin continued to be clammy and then turned very cold. Her emotions in turmoil, Susan left the room again.

"Let her be. Don't go in there," Don told Susan when she returned to the front room. A scowl twisted his face.

The bedroom had darkened. The only light came from where he and her mother were watching television. From the front room she hears Don's voice.

"You want to watch your favorite program, Ursula? It's Disney."

"No." Her reply was too weak to be heard. Don blocked out the light from the other room as he moved toward the bedroom door with Susan.

"You want to watch Disney?" he repeated.

"No. Tell Mommy I got to go potty."

Don turned on the bedroom light and saw Ursula. "I'm going to leave the house for a few minutes. I can't stand the sight of her."

Susan didn't even answer and instead lifted the young girl up in her arms and carried her into the bathroom. He followed, took hold of Ursula's lower lip, and pulled her mouth open. When he saw the raw, open sores that covered her mouth and throat he said, "Brush her teeth with salt water. Leave her on the toilet for a half-hour." He turned and left the room. A few minutes later the back door banged shut.

Ursula leaned back against the toilet tank. It took what small reserve of energy she had left to hold herself upright. Her mother turned and left her.

Susan felt compelled to go into her young daughter's bedroom. She stood at the door for several minutes just looking around. She entered and slowly fingered each doll, each toy that her child had not been allowed to play with in the past two months. She loved her little girl, but she loved Don more. If she didn't do what Don said he would leave her. She couldn't let him leave her. She opened the dresser drawer, pulled out a nightgown and a pair of panties, then turned and headed back to the master bedroom.

Ursula was tired, so very tired. She wanted to sleep--a deep, dreamless sleep. Her head fell backwards. Her skin was grayish in color, her eyes open and staring.

Susan entered the bathroom in time to see Ursula's head fall backward. She lifted the little girl up and went into the bedroom and carefully put her on the bed.

"Ursula," she cried out. "Ursula!" The child did not make a sound. "Do you want your daddy? Ursula, do you want your daddy?" She asked in a louder, more demanding, tone. Susan was scared, very scared. She reached over and placed her hand on the child's heart. She was relieved when she found it was still pumping.

She picked her up again carefully, and went into the front bathroom. She sat down on the edge of the tub with her child in her lap. Cradling Ursula in her arms, she leaned over and turned on the water faucets. She eased her child gently into the water and gathered her body. She lifted her back into her lap and swathed her in a towel. Again, she placed her hand over the child's heart and, again, she was rewarded by the feel of a weak heartbeat. Susan called Ursula's name over and over. Ursula did not answer.

Susan took her back into the bedroom and dressed her in her panties and a blue nightgown. She continued to call Ursula's name. Still the child did not answer. Her eyes remained open and staring.

Susan carried her from the master bedroom into the kitchen. She was desperate now. Even though she could feel the child's heartbeat, she was afraid. She had to do something to make her

51

well again. Earlier, she had made gelatin, and now she tried to feed it to her daughter.

Ursula's teeth were clenched shut. Susan couldn't open her mouth. Even as she held her she feared for Ursula's life when the child's head fell back. Susan again felt for a heartbeat. There was none.

It was 8:50 P.M. Ursula was dead.

Chapter 2

A Child's Death

Saturday Night

The back door opened and Don entered the kitchen. Susan looked up at him with grief-stricken eyes.

"She's dead," she cried out, "Ursula is dead!" Her face was white, her eyes were wide open. Don took the small child from his lover's arms and cradled her in his. He hugged her close to him.

"I love you, Ursula. Talk to me. Please talk to me!" he cried as he gazed into the child's staring eyes. Turning slowly, he went into the dining room and put her body on the floor. He started pacing, frantic at the turn of events. "Oh, God! Oh, God!" His eyes filled with tears and then overflowed. "I didn't mean it. I didn't mean it!"

He rushed over, picked up Ursula's body and carried it into the master bedroom and carefully placed it on the bed. He turned and asked Susan, "What are we going to do? We have to hide the body. You can tell the body has been abused. We could be arrested. Do you understand? We could be arrested!" He started pacing the floor again, running his shaking hands through his hair.

Susan watched Don. He had killed her child but she loved him and she had to help him.

"We could put her in the lake."

"There are too many houses around here. People would see us." He paused to think a moment. "Let's go to my friend's apartment. Maybe he will lend us his car. We could take her body somewhere and dump it."

They walked outside into a light, misty rain. The gate that led into the park next door should have been locked but the chain was old and rusted. They took the short cut through the park and walked around the iron horseshoe pitching pegs. The night was still. The frogs and crickets held their usual concert. The sounds of Don's and Susan's feet were muffled in the grass.

The blacker shape of the apartments loomed ahead, broken only by the scattered lights from the occupants who had not yet gone to bed. Don and Susan walked over to the apartments. He led her into the game room and they sat down on the couch.

They had been silent throughout the walk. Then Susan said to Don, an anxious look in her eyes. "Where are we going to put her if we get the car?"

"I don't know."

"We could throw her in the lake." Susan repeated her earlier suggestion in a quiet tone as if she was talking to a child. "Let's go get his car."

He got up without acknowledging her suggestion. Don took her hand and they both started walking toward his friends apartment. He stopped and stared at the apartment door.

Don had second thoughts. "Maybe involving him in this isn't such a good idea. What could I tell him without making him suspicious? We can't ask for his car."

They turned and retraced their steps. "Let's go look at the lake that's on the other side of these apartments."

Hand in hand they walked between the apartments and across the railroad tracks. They stopped at the edge of the lake and looked around.

"It's too big. We couldn't get out far enough unless we had a boat." Don observed as he stared at the lake. Silently, they turned and went back the same way they had come until they once again reached their house.

"There's a lake behind our house." Susan motioned to Don as they stood in their front yard. Together they moved toward the back of the house. They had to cross their backyard to get to an empty lot behind them. A two-story house stood to one side of their backyard. The house was dark and quiet. They crossed the street and entered the small space of grass leading down to the lake and another house.

"There are too many houses around here. Let's go look at the pond behind the apartments."

54

Once again they retraced their steps. First Don, and then Susan, climbed the fence that separated the park from the apartment complex. Once across, they had to walk around the pond until the growth surrounding it was sparse enough to push aside. Don bent down and picked up a small stone. He threw it into the middle of the pond and was satisfied with the splash he heard. The water was deep enough.

They turned and stood for a moment, waiting to see if anyone heard or responded to the noise they had made. The night seemed to have swallowed up the sound. Only crickets and frogs responded. When the noises of the night resumed, they carefully made their way back to the house.

Inside, Don told Susan, "Find something to put her body in." He checked throughout the house before heading out to the garage. Susan went with him. She did not want to leave his side, this man who had abused her daughter to death. He was her life-line. They rummaged together until Susan found a duffel bag. She held it up for him to inspect.

"It's too small."

They continued to look until Susan remembered the sail bag in her suitcase from her husband's sailboat. She went over to the suitcase, undid the clasps, and reached inside. Pulling out the white sail bag, she held it up for his inspection.

"What do you think?" she asked.

"It should do."

While they were in the garage he lifted up two eight–pound weights and a heavy-duty extension cord.

Susan touched his arm as they were about to leave the garage. She hesitated for a moment before looking up at him apprehensively.

"Don, I'm pregnant with your baby."

He shifted the weights and cord, putting them under his arm and freeing one hand. He patted the hand that lay on his arm and then grasped the weights again. His sharp face, for once, softened slightly.

"I'll make it up to you, losing Ursula that way."

They returned to the house and entered the master bedroom.

"Hold her while I tie these weights on," Don instructed Susan, his eyes not meeting hers.

She took her child's body in her arms and held her sideways while he put the weight against Ursula's chest. He took the extension cord and looped it around one hole in the weight and then wrapped the cord around Ursula's body. Susan held the other weight against the child's back, allowing him to tie it against the body with the electrical cord.

He looked down at the child he had abused, leaned down and kissed her on the forehead and then on her blistered lips. Susan continued to hold her child while he took the sail bag and pulled it over Ursula's head and over her body until it covered her feet. He yanked the drawstring tight. Lifting the bag up in his arms, he turned to leave the room. Susan followed.

They once again went through the park and to the fence separating the apartments from the park. The night was black. The rain had stopped and all was still. Susan climbed over the fence and then took her child from her lover's arms. She cradled the body while Don grabbed the cold steel fence and pulled himself up to the top. He jumped over, his feet making a dull thud in the quiet night. He helped Susan bear the weight of the child and together they walked toward the pond.

"I'll hold one end, and you hold the other. We'll walk in as far as we can and then we'll toss the body," Don whispered to Susan.

They waded into the pond. The water, warm from the day's sun, lapped at their feet. The water eased its way up to their ankles as they walked side-by-side into the pond. Susan started shaking and dropped her side of the bag. Don caught it before it hit the water. His curses were mere whispers in the night. Susan turned and moved back out, the slime oozing between the toes of her sandals as she reached the edge of the pond. Unable to completely walk away, she turned around and watched as Don continued to wade into the water until it was lapping around his hips. He raised the child's body above his head and heaved his burden away. It splashed into the silent pond scattering the few ducks that were swimming nearby.

"Don," Susan whispered anxiously, "a light just came on."

She pointed toward a house across the road from the pond. Don waded out of the pond, quickly took Susan's hand and hurried her away. They paused a few feet away on the grass, held their breath and waited.

No sound came from the house. No one investigated the noise. Hand-in-hand, they watched the bubbles that surfaced as the bag sank down to the bottom of the pond. The water rippled with circles until they widened and were no more. They turned and slowly walked back to the fence and climbed it, being careful not to make too much noise when they jumped down on the other side. They moved like shadows on the way back to the house. A light mist clung to their hair and skins as they hurried through the park, passed the gate into their own front yard, and into the house.

Silently, they locked up the house and turned out all the lights. Silence continued as they got ready for bed. Don held Susan close to him and tears formed in his eyes.

"Ursula!" Susan cried out.

"Forget about it."

"Her life was so short."

"Be thankful for the time you had with her."

Susan started to cry.

In the darkness Don whispered, "Don't cry, I don't want you to mention her death to anybody. Do you hear?"

In the wet, still night, at the bottom of a small retention pond, a child's silent cry went unheard.

Mommy, Daddy, it's cold down here. I don't like the dark, Mommy. I don't like being here. Why?

Sunday

Susan woke up. Awareness came to her. Ursula was dead. She wandered aimlessly through the house, passing Ursula's room. She shuddered and reached over to shut the door. Entering the front room, she stopped and stared at the beach towels that were still on the floor. She picked them up and quickly stuffed them into the hamper. Then she went into the kitchen and automatically made herself a cup of coffee.

Don and I have a lot to talk over. Is he going to leave me now? He has threatened to do it so often. He can't, I love him too much. He is the only man who has not abused me, or given me drugs, or got drunk every night.

She poured herself a cup of coffee and sat at the dining room table. She started to remember her life with Don.

She had met Don at the hotel where she worked. She had been dating someone else but her boyfriend had just announced his engagement to another woman. Even now she felt the same rage.

"How dare he bed two women at one time," Susan muttered to herself. Because she was mad at him she jumped at the chance to go out with Don. She never allowed herself to recognize her own affairs with other men.

Don was different. He didn't like drugs or alcohol, at least not to any great degree. She had been intrigued by him. It wasn't long before he and a friend of his moved into the house she was sharing with another woman.

That woman was a mess. Don and his friend changed all that. Like a whirlwind they went through the yard and cleaned it up, mowing and raking until it never looked better. Susan and her friend were made to thoroughly clean the inside by Don's demand.

Don brought Ursula toys and made her laugh and even took her places. What happened to make him change?

Gradually all of Susan's friends stopped coming over. He didn't like them because they supplied her with cocaine and he didn't want her to use drugs. He wanted her addicted to him instead. She did become addicted to him, although, not without a battle.

Susan remembered the time they had a fight. Don had yelled at her and finally threw his dinner at her. She retaliated by calling some "friends of a friend" who were instructed to physically threaten him and throw him out of the house. They

58

were hurt so badly in the fight that they had to go to the hospital. Don then had sweet-talked her out of being angry. He had stayed.

Soon they moved out of that house and into the house in Altamonte Springs, Florida—Ursula, Don, his friend, and Susan. Life was a little easier. Don was still sweet to Ursula. However, he was dealing in stolen merchandise because they needed the money. Neither one of them had a job.

It started to get a little scary when his younger brother and sister showed up. Don would get mad at the brother and Susan didn't like Don when he as mad. At least she had another woman around, but she couldn't get his sister to talk much about Don except to say she was afraid of him. Susan didn't understand why, until she witnessed the fights Don had with his friend and his younger brother. He beat up both of them. Soon it was only Don, Ursula, and herself in the house.

Money was tight so, she began to make phone calls for him. She was helping him fence stolen merchandise and even started going to flea markets, taking Ursula with her.

What she feared most had happened when the phone rang one afternoon. Don's friend had been arrested and the police were coming after them. They moved quickly, but not quickly enough. The police caught up with them at the end of the street and Don was arrested.

She recalled taking a television and some jewelry to a bail bondsman to get Don released. He had to lay low for a while so that meant she had to get a job.

He wasn't the same person anymore, she thought sadly. She loved him but she hated having to put up with his moods. He would be fine one minute and then cold toward her the next. She got so fed up with him she called her ex-boss at the hotel and asked him to come pick her up. He couldn't get away, so he sent a co-worker instead. When she came, Susan sent her to pack the things up in Ursula's room while she went to confront Don.

Susan shook her head sadly as she recalled how Don had persuaded her not to leave. He even went so far as to let her spend the night at the friend's house since she had been nice enough to come help. He came and picked up Ursula and Susan the next afternoon.

Later he became even harder to live with. He started putting Susan down, telling her she wasn't a good mother. According to him, she didn't make her child behave the way she should. He took over the disciplining of Ursula about two months before the child's death. He started keeping water from her. After that Ursula had to ask permission to go to the bathroom. That didn't bother Susan too much, but taking all Ursula's toys away until she obeyed him caused Susan to worry. Susan was afraid to question him fearing he would do what he had been threatening—pack up and leave.

He then began making Ursula stand in a corner for hours. One evening she stood until almost three o'clock in the morning, which left her too exhausted to attend school.

Susan, thought of the many nights he had abused her daughter.

"Why didn't I do something? Why didn't I get her out of here?"

She hated watching him beat Ursula so much that she often retreated to the bathroom and smoked a cigarette. He had even followed her one night yelling. "It's your kid! You discipline her, I'm fed up!"

She remembered he had stomped out of the bathroom, grabbed her daughter, pulled her into the bedroom, and in a rage started hitting her head against the wall. Susan's screams finally stopped him, as Ursula slumped down to the floor. He turned to Susan and started yelling at her again.

"I'm fed up! She's a brat! You should be disciplining her, not me."

It was half-an-hour before Susan was allowed to go to Ursula. Yet Susan was quick to obey when Don told her, "Take her into the front room and make her stand. Make her stand all night."

She waited until she thought he was asleep or at least drowsy, then took her daughter to her room and put her to bed. Unable to sleep, she paced the floor until she was exhausted.

The next morning, she remembered how he spoke to her in disgust. "You ruined my way of disciplining her," he told her.

When he stalked out of the house, slamming the door, she went into Ursula's bedroom and sat on the bed beside her child. Susan did not go to work and her daughter did not go to school, even though classes started that day.

Susan pulled her thoughts back into the present long enough to light one more cigarette. The ashtray was becoming full as she relived the months of August and September.

Ursula started school the next day. Don decreed that she could not come into the house after school. She had to go straight into the back yard and knock on the door if she had to go to the bathroom. Susan did not agree yet did nothing to interfere.

Susan knew that Don was still dealing in stolen merchandise and she understood that he didn't want Ursula to hear what was going on. Still she was disturbed when he started yelling, "Keep her out of my sight! I don't want her around me! She lies!"

The first two weeks in September were worse for Ursula. Don began hitting the child more frequently. It started with hard blows to the stomach when he would question her about drinking water or eating food at school.

The number and length of the times he made her stand increased. Often she was too tired to go to school. Then there were four days of peace, four days when Ursula was allowed to eat and sleep and attend school. It was during those four days that he threatened to leave. He told Susan, "I'm sick of you." On the fifth day, Don watched Ursula from the front room window until she wet her pants. The punishment started again.

Many times Susan would have to wait until he went to play ball to feed Ursula. It would be 7:00 PM or later before the child would eat her dinner. That was infinitely better for Ursula than when he stayed home and made her march around the house. Ursula often would be made to stand during meals. Her mother would feed her only after they had eaten. Then in the last week Ursula was alive, Don allowed her to have absolutely no food or water.

One incident stood out in Susan's mind above all others. She had come home from work and was delighted to find Don waiting for her at the front door. She remembered asking him about Ursula and being told, "She's sitting on the toilet," where Susan found her with a pair of wet panties pulled over her head, which Don stopped her from removing. She left her child sitting for over an hour with those wet panties over her head after being ordered to do so.

Susan's attention suddenly focused again, caught by the sound of running water. He was up.

> *They had to talk. Would he stand by her and their unborn child?*

Don came into the dining room.

"Don, what are we going to do?"

"What do you want to do?"

"You know we have to leave?"

"Yup."

"Should we get a motel room?"

"We have to sell the furniture first. Maybe you could get your friend to help us move?"

"I'll try," Susan murmured, unable to voice her real thoughts and fears. The days passed with both of them unable to comprehend or acknowledge what had happened.

Chapter 3

Fugitives on the Run

Susan and Don awoke but avoided each other's eyes. In silence, they went into the kitchen. Don leaned against the counter, his eyes cast downward, while Susan made breakfast. A cold silence continued while they ate.

Susan looked up at him, "We have to get rid of her stuff."

"We'll have to put it in some bags and throw it in a dumpster," he said in an offhand manner.

Their lease would be up in three days. They started working together to clean the house. Ursula's clothing, toys and bedding were the first items to be stuffed into bags. Don took them to the dumpster while Susan went to the store for empty boxes. They worked steadily throughout the day. They went through everything, packing what they wanted to keep and throwing away what they had no hope of selling. One section of the front room was piled high with boxes filled with items for storage. Other things were placed to one side that could be sold. Both worked in silence most of the time. They had nothing to say to each other.

Don stopped long enough to walk to the local store and buy a paper. When he returned, they sat on the couch and looked through the classified section until they came upon an ad that offered to buy house-loads of furniture. He went to the phone and called.

"It's all arranged, the men will be by tomorrow to look the stuff over."

They went back to work and continued until late into the night. Susan got up and dressed for work the next day. One day missed was all they could afford. She went through her normal routine automatically and tried not to think or feel. Her ride drove up about the same time as the truck from the second-hand store.

Don was able to sell all of the furniture and even some of the things from the garage. More important, he sold his weights to the man who helped load the furniture. Don and Susan never wanted to see those weights again.

The security deposit would come in handy once they had decided what they were going to do. For the moment they were drifting, allowing time to pass between their crime and making any sudden decisions.

Fear made them constant companions. Together, they went to the local laundromat. Together, they sponged down the blood-stained walls. They watched each other closely and constantly.

Susan continued to go to work as usual although she found it almost impossible to concentrate on her job.

On moving day, Susan asked a friend to help transfer the rest of their things to a motel in Winter Park, Florida. They arrived home from work and along with Don they loaded everything into the car and drove to the motel. Living in a small room was a real change from being in a large house.

The two conspirators were in danger when Susan was asked first by a neighbor and then by her friend, "Where is Ursula?"

"Lie," Don had told her, "Tell them she is in California with her father." She did as she was told—just as she always did. Each time she lied when asked. No one questioned her lie.

One night as they were sitting on their motel beds with the television blaring, Don broke their self-imposed silence. "I'm going my own way. What are you going to do?"

Susan looked at him in horror. After all that had happened, he was still talking of leaving her.

He couldn't! I won't let him! How can I stop him?

She pondered over the problem most of the night. The next morning she looked at him sadly and asked him, "Do you want me to get an abortion?"

Don looked at her in shock. Was she thinking of killing his child? Somehow he had to stop her.

"We don't have that kind of money."

After Susan returned to work, silence continued. They again sat in front of the television until they went to bed.

Susan's sobs awakened Don during the night. She had remembered the feel of her daughter's stiff, young body in her hands.

"Don't cry!" Don admonished her, "Don't think about it!"

After two weeks, it became too expensive to stay at the motel. They needed to find a more economical way to live. Unfortunately, Susan had quit her job because her boss had complained about her lack of attention to her duties as a waitress. He even accused her of behaving like she was "spaced out."

Don called a friend and asked if they could stay with him for a few nights. They moved from the motel into his apartment.

Susan and Don were becoming afraid of staying in the Central Florida area where they had committed their crime. How long would they be able to answer questions as to Ursula's whereabouts without anyone growing suspicious? They decided to go as far west as their finances would allow. The security deposit should have been paid to them but they couldn't wait any longer.

Don found Susan's old checkbook and insisted she go to various stores and cash checks on the account she had closed the year before. Money in hand, they boarded a bus for Daytona Beach to look for work.

Susan still feared that Don would leave her even though she continued to put up with his mental and verbal abuse. She felt stupid and unloved. Fear became her constant companion. She would not let him leave her behind. That very fear kept her from looking for work with any degree of success. Only once did she apply for a waitress position but with little enthusiasm and she knew she wouldn't be hired.

They stayed a week in Daytona Beach during which their relationship worsened. The coldness he had displayed before her child's death deepened.

They left Daytona Beach and took a bus to Ocala, Florida. They applied for work at a magazine company but within a few

65

days they became paranoid as they watched their boisterous co-workers. They worried constantly about being discovered.

Susan searched for a way to solve their need for money. She felt if she could make herself useful to Don, he would stay with her. She thought of someone she had met at the flea market who might be persuaded to send them enough money to return to Orlando. It wasn't long before they had the money and were on their way back to Orlando.

Susan had been busy cashing bad checks to accumulate money. They both agreed it was time to move on. Their plan was to head for Denver where Don could see his son and then go as far west as possible.

They boarded a bus and passed towns without noticing them. Tired and dissatisfied with each other, they got off in Atlanta and looked at a newspaper. It was hard to decide whether they were far enough away to stop and work for while or continue on. Their fear drove them back onto the bus and on the road west.

They got out at Nashville, St. Louis, and Kansas City. At each stop they tried halfheartedly to get work before once again boarding the bus.

Finally they arrived in Denver. Susan was bothered by Don's obsession with his ex-wife and child. His divorce had become final the day before Ursula had died. She wondered if the two events were connected.

Susan wanted Don to find work but he was more concerned about talking to his ex-wife. He contacted her on the second day in Denver.

"She said I could see the kids if I was going to stay around, but if I was only here for one night, forget it." He stomped around the room restlessly. "I'm going to the convenience store down the road. Be ready to leave when I come back." Susan went to the front desk of the motel and wrote another worthless check. They left again with the next stop in Reno, Nevada.

Once again, they got off the bus for a few hours. The same ritual was performed: they bought a newspaper, they discussed staying, and then decided to keep going.

They arrived in California, spent one night in an expensive San Francisco hotel and then went on to St. Helena to stay with a friend of Susan's. In the meantime, Susan had made arrangements to have the security deposit sent to them.

They had stayed five days in St. Helena and the check still had not arrived. Susan spent time watching television and playing cards with Don. He was still very cold toward her and didn't hesitate to use the threat of leaving whenever he got bored or frustrated with waiting.

She didn't think her friend would put up with them much longer so Susan called another friend in Los Angeles and they decided to go there. It was a long and tiring bus ride. Don wasn't even speaking to her now and her mind would often flashback to times spent with Ursula. Susan was beginning to wear down under the enormity of what she had allowed to happen to her child. Pressed against the bus window, she realized that Don was all she had. If she lost him now, she would be alone. Alone with her thoughts, her memories, and her conscience, she moved back toward him. She couldn't let him go no matter how he treated her.

Susan soon had to confront the inevitable questions from her friend.

"Where's Ursula?"

"She's in Orlando, with friends."

Would the time ever come when that question would stop being asked?

The first five days were spent in St. Helena trying to live with Don's icy personality. Only at night did he show her any warmth and then only as long as it took him to satisfy his own lust. The verbal abuse increased and yet she had no one else. He would not leave her. She would not allow it.

It was hard to look her friend in the face after five days. It was obvious Don didn't like Susan anymore. She tried to appease him by looking for work but at the end of another five days in L. A., they had to move on.

Don's cousin lived in the San Bernardino mountains and he let them stay for the weekend. A phone call to her cousin in Riverside assured them of a place for a few days but not until

Thanksgiving. She was hopeful that the check would have arrived by then. Why hadn't their landlord handed over the money yet? Would her friend be able to find them?

Moving from one town to another, under constant strain, living in fear of being arrested for murder, and her pregnancy all were wearing Susan down.

They went to a hotel in San Diego to wait two more days and then they could go stay with her cousin and be with her family.

Would they believe Ursula was with a friend in Orlando? Would they stand by her if they found out what she had done?

"I'm going my own way. I don't need you anymore," Don sneered at her.

"Don't you dare leave me! I'll tell them what you did!"

"What you let happen, you mean. You're in this as deep as I am. You're a drag! Do you know that? A drag!"

Susan's eyes widened and filled with tears and then she ran into the bathroom and locked the door.

"I love you," she shouted through the door, her voice cracking. "Do you hear? I still love you!"

Don and Susan hitchhiked the day before Thanksgiving to Los Angeles. When they arrived, her cousin hugged her and made her feel welcome. It felt good to be wanted again.

Don was on his best behavior during the holiday. It didn't last long as the verbal abuse worsened. Finally, after several days she went out and applied for a job in a restaurant.

Don was furious when she didn't get the job.

"You're an airhead! Worthless! You can't even get a lousy job, for God's sake!"

Where was the check? She made one more phone call to Orlando. Her friend didn't sound suspicious. Maybe Ursula's body hadn't been found yet. But the check was finally on the way. Now maybe Don would treat her better.

The next week Don surprised Susan. "I have to go to New York. You can't come. I can't help myself. I can't help you. I have to go to New York. I have girl friends there, O.K.?"

Susan went into a rage and slapped him in the face. Don picked up a shoe and threw it at her and it hit her and cut her cheek.

68

"I can't stand you anymore. I'm leaving. The last thing I need is a pregnant bitch hanging around my neck when I'm traveling," Don shouted at Susan while he threw clothes into a suitcase.

He's really going to leave me.

She shouted back at him, "You lousy son of a bitch! Don't you dare leave me! I told you what I would do if you left me. I told you!" She threw the other shoe at him. Stalking out of the room, she went in search of her cousin.

Finding her she hurriedly whispered, "I need to talk to you, but let's get out of the house first."

"Uh, yeah. Honey, Susan and I are going to get in the car and go get some milk," Susan's cousin told her husband. She turned to Susan and took her by the arm.

Don watched them leave, his faced filled with worry and suspicion.

Don told the husband shortly after the women left, "She hasn't been herself lately, you know. She's been having these weird dreams and fantasies. I don't want to lug a pregnant bitch around New York when I leave." He shoved his hands deep in his pockets as he headed for the backyard.

Susan turned to her cousin as soon as they were out of sight of the house. "Take me to the police station. Don killed Ursula."

Her cousin stared at Susan, and then drove as fast as she could to the nearest police station.

"I still love him, but he's going to leave me," Susan mumbled more to herself than to her cousin.

The bright lights of the police station temporarily blinded Susan as she entered. She stood for a moment and then shoved her way forward.

"I want to speak to some homicide detectives."

"I'm busy," the policewoman at the desk told her. "There are no homicide detectives available. I'm busy."

Susan would not be put off. It had taken all this time for her to gather up enough courage. Emphatically she demanded, "I want to speak to someone concerning a homicide!"

The policewoman motioned to several policemen. After a few words with her they took Susan by the arm and led her to a small room.

She looked around the starkly furnished room. Her over wrought nerves tightened until she felt she would scream. Three men entered the room and stood looking at her.

"My little girl is dead," she told them defiantly. "Don murdered my little girl."

Chapter 4

The Betrayal

The Riverside, California police officers saw that Susan's eyes were wide open, as if she was in shock. Terror filled her face as they led her to a small partitioned room away from the normal activity of the front desk. She broke out in loud sobs, "I'm afraid for my life. I'm afraid for my life. He's there right there in my cousin's house. He killed my child."

One of the officers told her, "Calm down. Just relax. I'm certain whatever is troubling you can be explained." Slowly and with great care they pulled the story from her.

Susan's emotions fluctuated from hysteria to composure. During the questioning her cousin stayed by her side. In one of her more intense moments Susan looked up, her face white with the emotions she was feeling and said, "I hate this baby I'm carrying. It would be better if it wasn't around anymore. Maybe I should do something that would just take care of everything."

The officers stood back and let Susan's cousin counsel and calm her down. Over and over again, she muttered, "I hate this baby, I hate it!"

The police continued to question Susan, trying to discover a hole in her story. Although she was extremely emotional— crying, agitated, and incoherent at times—she told the same story again and again.

"He killed my child. Don killed my child."

At last convinced that a possible crime might have been committed, they dispatched a car to pick up Donald McDougall.

Back at Susan's cousin's house, Don came in from the backyard to talk with the husband.

"Where did they go?" Don asked.

"I don't really know. Susie just came out and they took off for a ride somewhere."

"Well, did they go to a bar or something?"

71

"I doubt it."

"I don't like Susie getting drunk."

"So what?"

"She'll start screaming."

"Is she violent?"

"She starts telling weird stories."

"What do you mean by weird stories?"

"She tells bizarre stories and stuff when she gets drunk. She's going to call the cops."

"What would she call the cops about?"

"She's going to the cops with some weird story or something."

"Why would she call the cops if she is mad at you and wants you out of here? She's not going to call the cops and have you sticking around."

"I am leaving her and going back to New York. She is pregnant but I have rich girl friends in New York. They have offered me a thousand dollars to marry them. My chances are better in new York. I don't want to drag along some pregnant bitch. I need to call a girl in New York so I can get hold of another girl; she'll get me some money. There is a warrant out on me in Florida for jumping bail."

"What did they arrest you for?"

Don didn't answer but went into the kitchen, picked up the phone and placed his call. He hung up the phone and turned back to the other man with a smirk on his face—he had accomplished what he had set out to do. The husband began to feel that women were only objects to Don, that he really hated women and used them only for his own gain.

"I'm sorry I have to leave her like this, but she is in the way. These girls in New York won't treat me right if I bring her along. They'll send me money to come back to them and treat me right when I get there. I just don't need her."

Don looked out the window as a flash of light caught his eye.

Don's voice cracked as he said, "there are police out front." His face paled. "You're not going to let them in are you?"

"Well, the police can get in any time they like. Warrant or not. I'm not running a 'safe house' you know."

72

Don's body stiffened and he started to pace restlessly, sat down, and got up again.

A bang reverberated from the wall, the husband went to the front door and looked out. The yard was empty. Their large pet dog started barking loudly and its hair bristled. Again a loud bang reverberated against the wall.

"Here, hold onto the dog," he instructed Don. He waited until Don had the dog by the collar and then he opened the front door and went out. He heard guns being cocked and a rustle in the bushes. Police suddenly came out of the darkness with their guns pointed at him,.

"Are you McDougall?"

"No."

"Is he in the house?"

"I suppose so."

"Go get him."

"I live here. This is my house." He turned and went inside, afraid of the guns pointed at him.

"You got some friends outside, he said as he took hold of the dog's collar.

Don half-turned toward the back door. Do you think I ought to run?"

"Well, where are you going to go if you don't have any money? You won't go very far. If it is just for skipping bail, it won't do you any good. Stay here and face them. They will only catch you in the end."

"It's Susan. Susan called the cops." Resigned, Don turned back to the front room and stood waiting a moment before going out the front door.

Police surrounded him quickly, guns drawn and pointed right at him. They grabbed him, forced him to the ground and handcuffed him, and then put him in the back of a police car.

Don was brought into the police station and put into a holding cell. He was coldly unemotional, yet cocky and very sure of himself. Later in the evening he was taken into a small sound-proofed interrogation room. As Don sat down one of the officers turned on a tape recorder. The first officer asked him "Do you know why you were brought here?"

73

"No."

"Susan Assaid claims you killed her child, Ursula Sunshine Assaid."

"No! She is not dead, she is alive!" Don stated in a shocked voice. "I didn't do it. I didn't do anything."

"Do you know why Susan turned you in?"

"We are out of a job. It's very heavy-duty. She's looking at the situation that I am running out on her."

"And, all of a sudden, she walks in here," the officer prompted him.

Don was uncertain what to say. "All I know is ladies, O.K.? Like a lot of the guys on the softball team, we'd have a couple of beers, but I really, you know, I don't think I've ever released any feelings to a male, O.K.?"

"All you know is the ladies, right?"

"Yeah, right," Don said with a smile on his face. "There is no room for her in New York. She can take the bus ride with me, O.K. My uncle works for Greyhound, O.K. He's worked there for forty-two years. I'd probably get a freebie across the country and she could go with me. But these are the jealous type of girls in New York and they just won't put up with the stuff like she'll put up with. They're like, they'd throw me out with her."

"She has a place and it's with family. The holidays are coming and they're not going to bounce her out. She hasn't told them she's pregnant, O.K. So my whole scheme is—"

"Well, I just can't figure out what is going on here then," the officer said. "If you are not covering for her and the only problem you got is lack of money, then I don't understand why she is down here telling this story because it doesn't make sense. I thought it made sense when I thought this was just a lover's quarrel and this was a way to get you to stay here."

"She wants that tremendously, or she wants me to take her with me," Don declared.

"Who would know where Ursula is right now?"

"Sue."

"Sue says she thinks her daughter is dead."

"Yeah, but…"

74

"The last time you saw Ursula was when?"

"About the middle of September. I had a softball game and she went to the airport. She was going to see her father."

"What if I find her father and he says he hasn't got Ursula?"

"You got me, O.K.?" Don shrugged.

The officer changed his line of questioning. "Abused children become abusing adults. Is it possible that Sue did this? Is it possible that Sue abused her daughter and, in effect, killed her daughter without her knowledge?"

"No!"

"Why is it not possible?"

"Because I, at the time, I was not at work. I was at home all the time."

"You may have guessed this one wrong?" the officer questioned. "Would you take the blame for this girl?"

"No, no, no, no, no, no.!"

Don started talking in a rambling manner. "She got this job as a waitress. She doesn't talk much, but she has a sneaky way about her at times. She is a little bit of an airhead. Sometimes she is a little spacey, her eyes you just don't see anything, you know?"

"I mean there were a lot of times I didn't think she went to work and I'm not the type to call up, you know? And I'm not the jealous type. I'm pretty secure with girls and pretty confident about not losing them and stuff like that. But not murder, man, nah."

"Sue said you had abused your former wife's child unintentionally."

"I loved that girl!"

"Have you ever been questioned before?"

"I was arrested for making a false statement on an aircraft. It was sort of like a joke. It wasn't like a hijacking. It was a false statement on an airplane and I was arrested by the FBI. I received three years probation."

Don started to talk about Susan in a rambling manner again. It seemed he rambled on when questioned too closely about something he didn't want to discuss.

"Something mysterious, I think is the word. Most of the girls I would meet I would have pegged in a day or two, you know? But her, it's something eerie, something, something different, something mysterious, something, something that I couldn't put my finger on. Something that kept me thinking, kept me guessing. Those are the things I like. I like to investigate. I like to uh, uh, manipulate. I like to play head games with people and stuff and then, with her, I could never nail down her thoughts and stuff. I think that's what kept me with her. Sure, I love her, but I loved all my girl friends and I still do."

"Now Susan, doesn't impress me as being, now I am not knocking her, but she doesn't strike me as being the intellectual type or travel-oriented," the officer countered. "How are you guys intellectually matched?"

"Her knowledge? We're not very compatible, O.K.?"

"Maybe there was a physical attraction there?"

"No, no. There definitely wasn't a physical attraction there," Don stated emphatically.

The questioning continued. Don remained calm and denied the child was dead. If the child was not dead, he couldn't possibly have killed her. His calm demeanor was very convincing.

"Do you know Ursula is dead?"

"Nah, she's not dead."

"Have you talked to Ursula since she left?"

"She's not dead! She can't be dead, man!"

"I'm telling you right now that she is dead."

"NO!"

"Well you know this is a police department. We didn't call you down here to tell you fairy tales. You know the body's been located?"

"No! Don't say that! No! You got to find the husband. You're throwing a trip on me, man. I don't believe it happened. I don't believe it was done."

Finally, unable to break either of their stories, the police brought them together. The officer who had been questioning Susan cautioned her about staying strong when she confronted Don.

76

They entered the room and Susan kept her head up and tried to remain calm. The officer who had been interrogating Don, asked Susan, "In spite of the fact that he killed your daughter, you didn't want him to leave you?"

"I still love him a lot. But I've been having a lot of dreams about Ursula."

"You still love him in spite of the fact that he killed your daughter?"

"I started hating him a little bit the last couple of weeks."

"O.K. Is that all you want to say?"

Susan turned and asked Don, "Do you know of Ursula? Do you remember her?"

"Yes, Don replied.

"Well, where is she?"

"Ursula is with your husband."

"You're lying! You killed her! You're not going to get away with it!" Susan screamed.

"You're lying and crazy." Don answered. He stared at her as though willing her to be quiet. Susan faltered, dropped her eyes, and then lowered her head.

The officer who had been with Don from the beginning finally spoke up again, "Don don't stare at her. Susan, continue, but don't let him scare you."

Susan after a hesitant start, continued with her story. The officer who had interrogated Don asked her, "Why didn't you intervene and stop Don?"

Susan looked up. She stared at him a moment before answering. "I didn't stop Don because I loved him very much. He was the first man in my life that did not abuse me, did not use alcohol, and did not use drugs."

Don stared her down until she became silent.

"Why are you doing this to me?" He demanded.

"You murdered my daughter."

The officers, anxious to get to the bottom of this story, finally called the Altamonte Springs Police Department in Florida right after midnight and asked them to search for the child's body. Susan told the Florida police her story once again. She tried to tell them where the body had been thrown. The search started.

Unable to find the exact pond they called back at 3:00 A.M. to have Susan clarify and restate the location of the pond. The night grew long and boring while Susan and Don waited.

The Florida police searched for over two hours on a moonlit night before stopping until daylight, when they again entered the water and continued the search until the scuba equipment ran out of air.

While waiting for the tanks to be filled they searched the rest of the pond from a rowboat. At 11:15 A.M. they spotted a bag on the bottom in the northwest portion of the pond. A scuba diver entered the water and touched the bag. He could feel two objects that felt like weights and then felt a round object like a human skull toward the top of the bag.

Just before the bag was raised to the surface, a knucklebone fell from the sail bag. They retrieved the bag and bone, hauled it to the side of the retention pond and dumped it out.

A call was made to California. A police officer turned toward Susan and Don.

"They found her. They found the body."

"No! She's not dead. She is alive. You guys are kidding me." Don seemed astonished.

"They found her body. She is dead," the officer stated flatly, continuing to watch Don.

Don acted stunned and then grieved as if he couldn't believe Ursula was really dead. His eyes filled with tears. To the police in the room it was an almost believable performance.

Susan and Don were booked and held for extradition to Florida. Susan was startled when she found out they were going to hold her. She believed she would be set free.

As Don was led away he bent his head and cleared his throat as if to keep himself from crying, but quickly composed himself and raised his head high.

Chapter 5

Profile of a Child Abuser

The patterns of child abuse were revealed during the trial of Donald McDougall and Susan Assaid. Dr. Martin Lazoritz, a psychiatrist and child psychiatrist from Winter Park, Florida, was called as a defense witness. His testimony provided insights into Don and Susan's tragic behavior and also explored the actions of many child abusers.

Don and Susan's abuse of Ursula was a graphic example of the battered child syndrome, according to Dr. Lazoritz.

They had a distorted view of parenting because of the way they were raised. While there may be no single defined personality of an abusive adult, Dr. Lazoritz said, patterns of abuse can be traced from childhood.

Child abusers have never developed a basic sense of trust in other people, the sense of being close to other people, or the ability to get close, Dr. Lazoritz testified. As they grow up , they lead isolated lives, have difficulty being with other people, and have superficial sexual relationships. These factors together cause them to be very vulnerable to stress.

If this type of a person becomes a parent, Dr. Lazoritz speculated, there can be a strange role reversal. They give children powers that they don't have. They treat them as if they were adults and expect them to behave like adults. A child is expected to satisfy their emotional needs, to love them and almost take care of them.

Parents who have created this kind of role reversal will have unusual expectations of a child, Dr. Lazoritz said. For example, they may not be able to accept it if a child is not potty-trained by the time they are two years of age. Parents may become angry if the child doesn't have perfect table manners or interrupts conversations. They don't allow them to behave like children. They want them to act like adults. Adults expect too much because it was expected of them as children, along with the possible weak role of their own mothers in an unstable, chaotic family.

A child abuser has an immature personality, expecting the child to nurture them. Dr. Lazoritz testified that abusers are self-centered and believe the world revolves around them. An adult may use high self-image to hide feelings of inadequacy caused by terrible abuse as a child.

Most child abusers are chronically aggressive, frustrated, lonely, and mistrustful of others. Their thinking is rigid and they are not easily convinced that their behavior is wrong. Dr. Lazoritz found that they are frequently from broken homes, abandoned, often abused themselves, and have not formed close relationships with their own parents or with other people. Dr. Lazortiz concluded that a potential abuser expects too much from a child for their own emotional fulfillment.

Donald McDougall

Don was born in 1956 and was three years younger than Susan. His youngest brother and sister were afraid of him when they were growing up. His mother left the family when the youngest child was seven months old. She divorced their father and was awarded custody of the children, yet the children remained with their father. One of Don's brothers quoted him as saying, "I hate my mother because she left…"

His father was in and out of jail. He gambled and was an alcoholic. His father would make him ride around with him in his car all day, and because Don was not allowed to use the bathroom, he would end up holding himself.

Frequently, his father left the children in the care of his girlfriends. They too abused the children. Don was made to stand in a corner for long periods of time and was deprived of food.

Don called his family life "heavy-duty" which included a lot of abuse. One of his brothers described Don as an active, moody, and athletic boy. He relied heavily on his athletic ability to deal with his peers. He often tried to act as the father of the household.

During her testimony at his trial, Susan described Don as being changeable and moody. He was cold toward her and left her alone for days at a time. She felt he was unable to find sexual satisfaction with her. He brought other women to the house and would telephone other women as well as his ex-wife.

Don was married for two years to a woman with a four-year-old girl from a previous marriage. Don was quoted as telling his ex-wife, "You are not doing a good job in disciplining her." He hit the child if he felt she had spoken out of turn, had not eaten her dinner properly, or was sitting too close to the television. He would shove her and slap her in the face or backside. Often a slap was followed by a kick to whatever part of her body he could reach. He would make her keep soap in her mouth for half-an-hour and spit it out, then drink water and swallow whatever was left in her mouth.

There was much verbal abuse. He would tell the child, "Say one word and I'll cut your tongue out!" Another time, the child was playing in a tree and Don told her, "If you move or get down, I'll cut your feet off and eat them!" The child was ordered by Don to stand motionless from four to six hours. Later she was made to sit on the bed from lunchtime until midnight, without food or drink.

He would grab her arm and hold her over his head and throw her down on the ground. He would pick her up by the arm or hair, back of the head or neck and throw her across the room and bounce her off the wall.

Don's wife gave birth to a son and immediately Don demanded that the little girl no longer call him Daddy. The little girl still has mental scars and her mother said at the trial, "She remembers vividly everything he did to her." Two months after the birth of his son, Don dropped the infant three feet onto the bed because the child would not stop crying.

His wife left him three times because of his abuse of her daughter. After the third and final time, she applied for a divorce. The divorce became final September 24, 1982, the day before Ursula died.

According to police reports and F.B.I. files, Don had a long arrest record. One incident stood out. In July 1974, Don and two other friends boarded a plane and once it was airborne, told the stewardess, "I have a gun and we are going to Cuba." The horrified stewardess gasped, "You shouldn't talk like that!" Don replied, "I do have a gun and we will go to Cuba, I think." The stewardess backed away from him and went in to see the pilot. The plane was turned around and again landed in Texas. He was charged with air piracy and received three years probation.

He also resisted arrest after being stopped for a traffic violation and was charged at various times for grand theft and possession of stolen property.

His two-week trial for the death of Ursula Assaid was held in October 1983 in Clearwater, Florida. He pleaded guilty to two previous bad check charges but innocent to the charge of second- degree murder.

During the trial, Don acted in an offensive manner, giving what he thought of as the "evil eye" to the prosecuting attorney and made obscene gestures to the judge and Susan. He tried to stare Susan down in hopes of getting her to stumble over her testimony.

When the defense called Dr. Martin Lazoritz, he testified that Don did not always cooperate with testing because he was afraid of what would come out. Psychological tests proved he had a personality disorder and was suffering from anxiety and depression. Dr. Lazoritz described him as a defensive person with an immature personality. He had difficulty with relationships, with sexuality, and was unsure of himself as a male role model. He felt inadequate, was disorganized in his thinking, and lacked self-identity.

"Now, relating this back to his history, would it be consistent with his being an abused child?" Don Marblestone, the prosecuting attorney, asked Dr. Lazoritz.

"Yes, certainly."

"What would cause him to do the type of behavior he did toward Ursula?"

"In part from his development, some of these things were from his experience and personal profile," Dr. Lazoritz said.

82

"He would think of this as a form of discipline. He would become an authority figure, higher than a father figure, and improve his self-image."

"Would you have an opinion as to what the reason might be for making a child do these types of things?" Dr. Lazoritz was asked.

"One reason would be the sense of having to make the child to conform to what he thought were valid rules of behavior. He thought that the way to do it was to utilize the things that were done to him. That was one thing. Another thing, is that his being 'in charge' made him feel better about himself in a weird sort of way."

Marblestone continued to ask about Don's patterns of abuse.

"If he tried to get the child to talk about a fantasy figure she had, and tried to get her to realize she was bringing it out in the open so he could change her thinking, would it give you any insight into—"

"Well, it would be consistent with what I was just saying. To get the little child to confide in him, to be able to help her, would make him feel better about himself. The other possibility he too had something similar in his childhood."

"If he told someone else," Marblestone continued, "Hey, I'm making this kid stand up all weekend. She wets her pants so we don't give her any water or give her any food. And she lies, I make her eat soap." Is there any significance to him telling this to someone else?"

"With that kind of personality, he wouldn't want himself to look bad," Dr. Lazoritz said., "so he must have thought he was doing something good in a very dis torted way. The personality profile shows he has very unusual perceptions or thoughts. He wouldn't want to make himself look bad because he had a poor feeling about himself. He thought of these things as good, even though it was horrible to everyone els e. He thought it was good, that they were helpful to her and teaching her how to behave."

"Is Mr. McDougall a sane person?" Marblestone asked.

"I would consider him sane."

"In this case, does it indicate Don would be a manipulative type person and have control over others?"

"He was abnormally manipulative," Dr. Lazoritz pointed out. "He would do anything he could to make himself look good so people would look up to him. In a relationship with women, he would like to be looked up to, be in charge, be adored and worshipped. It is all distorted and disturbed. He is capable of lying and lying consistently. He would tell others about the abuse, thinking he had done right in correcting the child."

Susan Assaid

Susan Barrett Assaid was born in New Zealand in 1953, and became an American citizen when she was eight years old. Her mother divorced her alcoholic father the same year. Susan was not allowed to see her father after the divorce.

After her mother remarried, when Susan was ten years old, Susan's stepfather started to beat her. He would hit her in the mouth and stomach with his fists, beat her with a belt, and kick her. When he was going to discipline her he often made her take off her underpants.

Susan showed her mother the bruises, but she did nothing. Most of the time her mother stood by and passively watched the beatings. Only once did her mother intervene—he was pounding Susan's head into a wall, she was bleeding and her mother hollered for the stepfather to stop. Afterward, Susan was not taken to the doctor. Often she had to stand at attention for an hour or two. She was made to holler, "Yes sir!"

Susan would ask her mother if she could stay at a neighbor's house when the beatings got too much for her. Even though she would stay with the neighbor, the abuse was never reported. She escaped the beatings when her stepfather passed out in an alcoholic stupor. She ran away from home when she was 12 – years-old because of the beatings but returned home the next day. She told her mother she had run away because of the beatings, but again her mother did nothing to stop them. She claimed to have run away again at age fourteen, when she was forced into a car and raped. Lie detector tests showed she lied about being raped.

Susan also started using drugs when she was fourteen. After starting to smoke marijuana, she went on to use cocaine, LSD, mescaline, Quaaludes, and amphetamines.

At age sixteen, she reported her stepfather's abuse to police who she claimed told her she deserved to be beaten. She ran away again and claimed she was raped once again. This time, she did not report it to the police.

Susan married in 1974 when she was twenty years old. Her husband did not stay at one job long and they lived at various times in California, Maryland, Miami, Atlanta, back to Miami, and then back to California. While in Miami they lived on a boat they had bought. Susan kept the sail bag with her from that boat—the one in which Ursula's body was wrapped.

Susan claimed that her husband began to use and sell drugs and that he encouraged her to use them. He would call her "Susan I" and "Susan II" because sometimes she had a calm and sometimes an irrational personality due to heavy drug use.

When Susan was pregnant her husband did not want the child and asked her to have an abortion. Susan refused, stopped using drugs, and a healthy child was born in 1977. Her husband was delighted with the child and said she looked just like sunshine. He wanted the baby to have the initials U.S.A. and named her Ursula Sunshine Assaid.

Her husband's drug business scared her enough to purchase a gun. She also feared her daughter would see Quaaludes and cocaine on the coffee table and put them in her mouth. It was the main reason Susan left her husband.

In 1979 Susan and Ursula stayed with her husband's grandmother in Florida for about three months. Eventually, Susan and Ursula rejoined the husband in California. However, her husband decided he did not want to live with her. The day her husband left her, Susan forcibly tried to prevent him from driving the car out of the garage. Susan and Ursula then moved in with her husband's employers and found out her husband was dating someone else. Susan became angry and called his girlfriend, threatening her and calling her a prostitute. At the time, Susan was having sex with the son of her husband's employer.

Susan sold everything they had without her husband's knowledge. She then took an additional amount of money from him and returned to Orlando with Ursula. She stayed with a former lover, a man she had met in San Jose who was playing in a band at a local Orlando restaurant. She liked to listen to the band practice but often felt Ursula was in the way. If the child interfered too often, she would shut her in her dark bedroom and ignore the child's cries.

Susan ended that relationship and moved into a friend's home with another woman who kept her supplied with cocaine. Susan started dating and enjoyed partying. During the next year, Susan worked at two Orlando area hotels. She moved into the home of her first boss to help take care of his children and the house. He eventually asked Susan to leave his home when he met another woman he had decided to marry. Susan then moved in with Ursula's day-care teacher and her four daughters. Susan met Don at the hotel in December of 1981 and Don moved in with her one week later.

The Sentencing

Donald McDougall was found guilty of second-degree murder and a lesser count of aggravated child abuse by a twelve member jury after they deliberated for seven hours. The maximum sentence in Florida for aggravated child abuse was five and one-half years, but he was sentenced to double the maximum time for aggravated child abuse, equaling eleven years, and double the maximum time for second-degree murder. The worthless check convictions were one year each, making the maximum sentence thirty-four years.

The judge went beyond the guidelines in the second-degree murder conviction for four reasons:

1. The defendant was particularly cruel to the victim, and caused considerable pain and suffering resulting in the death of the child.

2. The cruelty occurred over an extended period of time and that involved planning and deliberation.
3. The child was particularly helpless because she was five years old and because her mother didn't intercede in the abuse.
4. McDougall was in charge of the child's discipline, and McDougall had a severe personality disorder.

Donald McDougall was sentenced on November 4, 1983 to thirty-four years at the Seminole County Correctional Facility in Sanford, Florida. He would be eligible for parole in fifteen years.

On February 12, 1985, the Fifth District Court of Appeals upheld the guilty verdict and the thirty-four year prison sentence for Donald McDougall.

Earlier, on March 24, 1983, Susan Assaid pleaded guilty to the charge of manslaughter in the death of her daughter, Ursula. Prior to sentencing, her lawyer told the court "Susan is not a monster and is not some socially deviate human being that lacks the capability to live in our society, but a victim as well." He said that "in her relationships with men she is 'totally submissive' and did not understand that psychological domination and control can only cause pain and hardship. She didn't stop it from happening when she had the opportunity to do so."

Susan was sentenced to 15 years imprisonment and she agreed to testify in the trial of Donald McDougall. She was denied parole in 1985, and she was released from the Broward Correctional Institution on July 14, 1988.

Susan's child by Don McDougall was born in 1983. It was ruled that Susan and the boy's father had permanently lost all rights to the child. The child was taken out of state and the adoptive parents would never be allowed to find out the details of his background.

The penalties for child abuse resulting in death were also tightened in the state of Florida. The assistant prosecutor at the McDougall trial, Donald Marblestone, led a public campaign for a first-degree murder penalty which became a Florida state law in 1984. He said child abuse death should have "the same penalty as if the victim's death were intended by the defendant."

Someone Heard

Orlando resident, Melanie Arrington read about the trial of Don and Susan and was outraged.

"I read it and was totally shocked. I was sitting there, I was warm, I was comfortable. I had a full stomach. No one was beating me, beating my kids, torturing me. I was just extremely upset that something like this could happen on our doorstep and no one knew about it. I decided I wouldn't stand for it. Something was going to be done. People needed to know about this. There wasn't enough community awareness out there."

Arrington started a memorial fund for the dead child which grew into the Ursula Sunshine Child Abuse Prevention organization. With Florida State funding, "The Sunshine Connection" project was set up to counsel and educate first-time parents, including teenagers in Seminole County, Florida. The organization was in existence for several years and made a significant contribution to the families of Seminole County.

Publisher's Note:
Arrington also brought together a group of writers and suggested they chronicle the tragic events that led to Ursula's death. Eve Krupinski and Dana Weikel were the two writers that completed the difficult task of pouring through trial transcripts and writing the story from the child's perspective.

The Circle of Violence

Epilogue

A killer's legacy—two lost lives and tougher child abuse laws

(Reprint from October 1996 *Jacksonville Magazine*
Randy Noles, Publisher)

Donald McDougall, killer of Ursula Sunshine Assaid, died on Monday, October 1, 1996 when a fellow inmate at the Avon Park Correctional Institution in Polk County, Florida clubbed the 40-year old child murderer to death with an iron spike used for games of horseshoes.

McDougall was serving a 34-year sentence for the 1982 murder in Orlando of 5-year-old Ursula "Sunshine" Assaid, the daughter of his live-in girlfriend, Susan Assaid. He would have been released in 1997, if not for the 33-year-old Arba Earl Barr—who was already serving a sentence for robbery and aggravated battery, an now faces a first-degree murder charge.

Ursula's slaying received national attention because of both its unusual brutality, and the fact that scores of people had reason to believe that the child was being abused, yet did nothing to stop it.

In her final few tragic months of life, Ursula was beaten, denied food and water, fed soap, not allowed to sleep and forced to stand naked for hours and recite the alphabet.

When she finally died after a particularly savage beating, McDougall and the girl's mother—who admittedly did nothing to stop the ongoing torture—bound Ursula's broken body and dumped it into a retention pond.

Susan Assaid pled guilty to manslaughter in 1983, and was released in 1988. She was last reported living quietly in South Florida and has borne another daughter. McDougall, however, was convicted of second-degree murder, aggravated child abuse, and writing bad checks.

But the story, thankfully, didn't end with McDougall's incarceration.

Christine Crosby and Judy Fontenot, partners in a small publishing company in Orlando, Florida were presented with a manuscript by a local writer, Ruth Paton. Paton was a friend of the two writers who had authored a manuscript documenting the last five days of Ursula's life.

Together, these women dedicated their time, energy and considerable money to child abuse prevention and education. Calling upon her considerable marketing savvy and genuine passion, Crosby persuaded major grocery chains to stock the chilling paperback. She distributed the book through schools where it has, at times, been required reading—and to government agencies and corporations.

Death From Child Abuse...and no one heard has been read by hundreds of thousands of people across the country and the world over. And because the book contains tips on recognizing child abuse and a comprehensive child abuse resource directory, it is safe to assume that its publication may have actually prevented tragedies similar to Ursula's.

The case also spawned changes in Florida law. McDougall might have already been a free man, if not for a change imposed on a 1995 law requiring prisoners to serve at least 85 percent of their sentences. The law was expanded to become retroactive, largely in response to media reports that McDougall would otherwise be released.

Also, at the time of McDougall's trial, the state could not seek the death penalty because state law required prosecutors to prove the crime was pre-meditated. That is no longer required in cases involving death from child abuse. In addition, so-called "crowding credits", under which felons could shorten their sentences as a result of prison overcrowding, were eliminated for prisoners who committed violent offences.

As a result, thousands of Florida's most contemptible predators have spent more time behind bars than they would have, had it not been for McDougall's notoriety. That—combined with the fact that even other inmates despise child killers—made McDougall a marked man behind bars. While no one should consider a thug like Arba Earl Barr a hero, at least he accomplished what our justice system could not—he assured that Donald McDougall would never hurt another child. The bottom line: A little girl is dead. The man who killed her is now dead, too. If any tears are to be shed, shed them for Ursula "Sunshine" Assaid, a precious 5-year-old who needed our help when we were otherwise occupied, unable or unwilling to get involved.

We weren't listening then, but we're listening now.

PART TWO

You Can Help Stop
Child Abuse
And
Domestic
Violence

Chapter 6

Child Abuse and Domestic Violence

Recognizing the immense problem of child abuse and domestic violence and helping improve the lives of children and families—is what the story of Ursula Sunshine is about.

Lucy Braun, former Orange County, Florida, Child Abuse Prevention Coordinator and licensed mental health counselor, offers her insights in this chapter. She has taught many professionals about the warning signs of child abuse and how to counsel those involved in abuse cases.

Child abuse is not new and it did not begin in this century. Children have long been regarded as "belongings" with an obligation to grow up and meet parental expectations. These expectations may be realistic, reasonable, and provide a sound healthy framework for a child to thrive. Unfortunately, many parents use dysfunctional parenting methods which they learned from their own parents or they developed from a lack of knowledge, perhaps to compensate for the stresses of their own lives. Some parents do not realize that they are being abusive and their children do not comprehend that they are being abused.

In 1966, Dr. Henry Kempe, founder of the International Society for the Prevention of Child Abuse and Neglect, described the "battered child syndrome." This medical term identified children with injuries not attributable to natural causes or true accidents. These children have suffered serious injury at the hands of their parents or parent-substitutes.

The tragic case of Ursula Sunshine shows what can happen when parents have had poor parental models, multiple problems, chronic stress, and little knowledge of available resources. Reading the account of this child's last few days

93

provokes horror, anger, disbelief, and a sick feeling that defies description. It is important to remember that not all child abuse is this horrific. Most abuse of children is much more subtle but is extremely damaging to the child and often has long term harmful effects on them, their children and society at large.

Child abuse is a cancer in our society. Violence breeds violence. Why has this cycle been allowed to continue? How did it remain hidden? In large part, prevailing societal attitudes were to blame. The long held belief, that what went on within the home was private and of no concern to others, created an atmosphere in which abuse could thrive.

The first effort to protect a child by legal intervention in America was in 1874. "Little Mary Ellen" was a nine-year-old girl indentured to Francis and Mary Connolly. She was being whipped daily and stabbed with scissors while tied to a bed. Neighbors repeatedly reported the incidents to authorities, who considered it a private matter, and did not interfere.

Etta Wheeler, a concerned, caring woman did not relent in her struggle to rescue the child from her tormentors. She turned finally to Henry Bergh, an official of the Society for the Prevention of Cruelty to Animals (SPCA). He appealed to the court on the basis that the child, as a member of the animal kingdom, was entitled to "at least the same justice as the common cur."

Mary Ellen was removed from the home and Mrs. Connelly was sentenced to a year in prison. The child was adopted by a new family and with the nurturing she received, began to thrive. (Pictures of the girl, before and after her abuse, still hang in the offices of the New York SPCA, along with the scissors with which she was tortured.)

Abuse is a problem for all of us, not just the victims and their families. Our prisons are literally bursting at the seams with victims of abuse who have become perpetrators of crimes against society. A high percentage of violent offenders have some history of abuse or neglect. Billions of tax dollars are spent each year to maintain prisons, law enforcement, and hospital facilities in the battle against societal problems caused by abuse.

Are we losing the battle against child abuse? Are weapons of punishment, retribution, and fear effective in preventing parents and other caregivers from harming children? What else can be done without the government violating personal privacy? What can one person do to help?

What is Child Abuse?

Child abuse is an action or series of actions inflicted upon a child that causes harm and leaves scars. These scars can be physical, emotional, or spiritual and may not be evident to the casual observer. Abuse damages bodies, minds, self-esteem, relationships, and family systems.

Most experts agree that abuse and neglect can be categorized as physical, sexual, or emotional abuse, or neglect. Some cases involve more than one, or sometimes all of them.

Physical Abuse

Evidenced by bruises, broken bones, burns, abrasions, cuts, bites, and other physical injuries that need medical care. These injuries are inflicted to make a child comply with expectations, to punish, or perhaps to show dislike for the child.

Physical Indicators of Physical Abuse
Unexplained Bruises and Welts

- on face, lips, mouth
- on torso, back, buttock, genitals, or thighs
- on several different surface areas of the body
- on neck from being choked or strangled
- on scalp with hemorrhaging
- on infant, anywhere
- on upper lip from forced feeding
- wounds resembling outlines of object used to cause injury
- absence of hair in patches on scalp
- traumatized ear lobes

lesions in various stages of healing that regularly appear broken, chipped, or missing teeth

Unexplained Burns
♦ cigar or cigarette burns, especially on soles of feet, palms of hands, back or buttocks
♦ immersion burns (sock-like, glove-like, doughnut shape) on buttocks or genitalia
♦ "dry" contact burns which show mark left by instrument used to inflict injury
♦ rope burns on arms, legs, neck, or torso

Unexplained Fractures
♦ fractures of nose, skull, jaw, or other facial bones
♦ bone separations indicating pulling or jerking
♦ rib fracture in child of preschool age
♦ swollen or tender limbs
♦ fractures in various stages of healing

Unexplained Lacerations, Abrasions
♦ of mouth, lips, gums, eyes
♦ of external genitalia
♦ on backs of arms, legs, torso

Behavioral Indicators of Physical Abuse

Behavior in children that is well out of the ordinary warrants investigation. The following are indicators of physical abuse that may also appear as the result of other emotional trauma. Abuse, physical or otherwise, should be considered as a possible cause when no other reasonable cause can be determined.
♦ Is wary of contact with adults
♦ Seems frightened of family members
♦ Becomes apprehensive when adult approaches another child who is crying

♦ Demonstrates extremes in behavior such as extreme withdrawal

Sexual Abuse

Includes any inappropriate sexual interaction with a child either physical or nonphysical and includes any attempts to exploit the child sexually. Incest, rape, and sodomy are violent forms of abuse but exposing body parts, suggestive talk, and subjecting children to degrading sexual innuendo are also abusive. Some young victims are used to produce pornography or forced to become child prostitutes.

Things Parents Should Know

- Who your child's friends are, where they live and what their phone numbers are. Meet the parents of your child's friends
- Who your children are spending time with and where
- Any gifts or items that your child comes home with
- Any strong bonds your child is developing with an adult

Things Children Should Know

There are individuals (male or female) who sexually prey on children. They may or may not be related to the family. They may or may not be a friend of the family. You can help reduce the risk of your child being a victim of a sexual offender if they are taught:

- No one has the right to touch the private parts of their body, or ask them to touch their private parts.
- They should tell their parents or a trusted adult if anyone asks to take their picture or give them gifts.
- They should not get in a car driven by a stranger.
- They should never go into an adult's home without their parents or guardian knowing about it.
- They should not answer the door when they are home alone.

- They should not tell anyone over the phone that they are home alone.
- They should tell their parents or trusted adult if anyone tries to talk to them about sex.
- Adults do not normally have "best" friends that are children.
- If they are uncomfortable in any situation, they should remove themselves from that situation immediately and tell a parent or trusted adult.

Pedophiles

Pedophiles are people who are obsessed with children. Beneath the surface of their personality they harbor a strong drive to have sex with children. This type of child molester may appear to be a genuinely caring person who really loves children. Pedophiles typically prey on only one gender and often children of a specific age. Many are very patient, sometimes working on a child's belief in them for months prior to any actual contact. They may take their victims to special places, buy things for them, and give them special time and attention. In "shopping" for victims, the child molester will often seek out children who need adult attention. Children of recent divorce or separation and children whose parents both work are frequent targets.

Physical Indicators of Sexual Abuse

- bruises around the mouth of infants
- torn, stained, or bloody underclothing
- difficulty in walking or standing
- complaints of pain or itching in genital area
- genital injuries such as lacerations, swelling, bruises, bleeding
- bruises or bleeding in external genitalia, vaginal, or anal areas
- vaginal and anal tears
- bruising or laceration of the penis or perineum, venereal

sores, anal ulcers or vaginal discharge
- difficulty with urination
- venereal diseases, especially in preteens
- physical complaint with no apparent basis
- pregnancy

Red Flags – The Warning Signals of Sexual Abuse

Sexually abused children manifest a wide variety of generalized and more specific (sexually related) signs of emotional trauma. Some children may present an entire constellation of symptoms, while others may elude even the most sensitive and well-trained eye. Any one or even a few symptoms may not necessarily be an indicator of sexual abuse.

Psychosomatic Complaints

Sexually abused children may present to the teacher, guidance counselor, school nurse or parent complaints of recurrent, specific or non-specific aches and pains. These symptoms may resolve after disclosure of the sexual abuse or incest within the family. If sexual abuse is suspected the child should not be interviewed about the abuse. Rather, a trained interviewer should be identified who has experience in this kind of work. A medical examination is recommended to rule out more serious physical problems and to aid in the determination of the actual problem. In some cases, there is medical evidence indicative of sexual abuse.

- vague headaches
- stomach aches, abdominal pain
- dizziness
- nausea, loss of appetite
- anxiety reactions
- chest pain
- difficulty breathing
- difficulty urinating
- complaints relevant to the genital or anal region

Sexually Related Behaviors – Sexual "Acting Out"

Exploring sexuality is a normal part of childhood. Inappropriate sexual knowledge or behavior is a possible indicator of sexual abuse. The phrase, sexually acting out, is often used to describe a wide variety of behaviors commonly observed in sexually abused children. In young children, most frequently alluded to are pelvic thrusting movements and simulated intercourse using dolls, toys, animals, or other children as sex objects.

Sexually stylized or "seductive" behavior in young children may be an indicator of abuse. A child who strikes poses, assumes mannerisms or repeats phrases that are sexually provocative may have learned that these behaviors lead to (and may be their only means to) attention, rewards, and love.

Children today certainly appear more precocious in general than ever before. They are constantly barraged with extremely provocative stimulation through the media. However, graphic and detailed stories or depictions of sexuality including oral sex, vaginal and/or anal intercourse, etc. from a child normally developmentally too young to be aware of the degree of detail described are a possible sign of sexual abuse.

Excessive or Compulsive Masturbation

Often we hear the question, "How do we know when masturbation is excessive?" Masturbation is normal. Excessive masturbation may be visible, frequent, disturbing, distracting, repetitive behavior. It is difficult to ignore. It may be an unconscious attention-calling device to a serious problem. Generally, in normal school-aged children, the socialization process has inhibited such persistent behaviors.

Psychological Dynamics
Family Indicators of Sexual Abuse

As in any overview, the following characteristics are more a composite of many cases than absolutes for every incestuous family. However, in reviewing cases, certain familiar attributes do seem to emerge over and over again. Often these patterns are more easily recognized in retrospect.

The denial of incest by children who are asked directly is a most common occurrence. The child will often retract and deny their initial admissions even after detailed reporting to appropriate individuals. Their fear of reprisals, guilt and confusion, and in many cases pressure placed upon them in the home, causes this ambivalence so commonly observed.

Isolation

Incestuous families may exhibit a higher degree of social isolation, whether living in an isolated rural area, the inner city, or suburbia. The parents rarely have trusted peers or activities that take them outside the home. There appears to be little intimacy with others. They may seek isolation in an effort to prevent their behavior from being discovered by others. The incest offender often overprotects the child in a similar effort to maintain the secret.

Role-Reversal

There may appear to be a reversal of traditional family structure in the incestuous family: the child acts like a parent and the adult exhibits infantile coping mechanisms toward his/her parental role. The child is often burdened with many of the parental responsibilities for the family. Mother/daughter role reversal is common: the daughter is overly concerned with protecting ("mothering") her own mother, a pattern that underlies the motivation for keeping the incest a secret.

Prior Abuse

The father and/or mother may have been sexually, physically, or emotionally abused themselves as children. Males who were sexually abused may victimize children in an unconscious effort to resolve their own abusive experiences. It is common for abusers to later rationalize their responsibility for the abuse by blaming their victims.

101

The Child Victim of Sexual Abuse

Females who were abused as children may internalize their victimization by suffering from diminished self-esteem, developing passive, overly-compliant personalities, or seeking abusive spouses (modeled after their own abusers) who reinforce their already-poor self concepts.

The role-reversal described above often leads to a behavior in the victims known as "pseudo-maturity." The parents look inappropriately to these children to fulfill their needs; the children have the weight of the world on their shoulders. They begin to worry not only about how next month's bills are going to be paid but also how to keep father, stepfather, mother's boyfriend away. This pseudo-maturity has also been referred to in the literature as the "betrayal of innocence," a false maturity in a child too old for their years.

Males who were abused as children may react somewhat differently than females. Boys, too, may initially internalize their victimization and suffer from poor self-esteem and depression. However, these feelings of depression and negative emotional flooding are often overwhelming. Boys at this point, as a way to protect the integrity of their self, may begin to act out or externalize their feelings, whereas girls tend to act in and internalize, often taking some form of somatic expression. Boys will tend to express these feelings through extreme aggression, vandalism or other acts that place the locus of the pain outside of themselves.

The following are common responses of males to sexual assault. It is important to note that these symptoms may occur as the result of many other types of emotional stimuli, including physical or emotional abuse.

➤ Drug and/or alcohol abuse
➤ Aggression
➤ Exaggerated stereotypical masculine behavior
➤ Self-hating or self abuse
➤ Eating disorders
➤ Depression
➤ Fear of Abandonment

- ➢ Sexually transmitted diseases
- ➢ Gaps in memory
- ➢ Low self-esteem; feeling on the brink of failure
- ➢ Anxiety
- ➢ Withdrawal
- ➢ Feeling guilt or shame when receiving touch
- ➢ Feeling detached from his emotions or his body
- ➢ Sexually acting out or avoiding sexual relationships
- ➢ Sudden changes in behavior and/or personality

Note: not all abuse victims have the same experiences, nor do they have the same reactions to those experiences. With appropriate help, any child can overcome their negative feelings and have a fulfilling and successful life.

The Mother

The mother-daughter bond in incestuous families is generally weak, and the mother may be emotionally withdrawn from the family. She may feel exploited by her husband or boyfriend. A high percentage of incest victims' mothers were also abused as children. Unfortunately, she is often blamed for the abuse perpetrated by the offender himself.

There are instances when the mother is consciously or unconsciously aware of the incest, yet finds herself without the insight or skills to deal with the problem. She may repress her suspicions to protect herself from childhood memories of her own abuse. She may have a great investment in maintaining the status quo, the appearance of normality in her family.

Fear of exposure, humiliation, personal harm, or financial deprivation, may serve to increase the mother's inability to protect her child. Too often the protection of the child suffers as a result of the process of the mother's own victimization.

The Incest Offender

The notion that incestuous fathers, stepfathers or grandfathers are highly sexed and aggressive men is generally false. Although some incest offenders may appear extremely domineering and authoritative in their homes, hey may be passive and ineffectual individuals outside the family. Their negative self-concepts, low self-esteem, and general feelings of inadequacy are conducive to their adoption of behavior that is destructive to themselves and others.

The incest offender often rationalizes his parental responsibility to the child in order to satisfy his own unmet needs for affection, companionship, and sexual gratification. He may tie his victims into a self-serving relationship by manipulating their needs for affection, love and attention. It is common for offenders to be in denial of their responsibility for the abuse. Often they will blame the victim, claiming "seductive" behavior etc, was the cause of the abuse.

It is becoming more evident that, in many cases, perpetrators of incest seek victims outside the home as well.

Exposure: A Time of Crisis

The exposure of incest, whether intended or inadvertent, usually precipitates a serious crisis within the family. Family members generally experience feelings of shock, fear, anger and confusion. The appropriate concern of the professional involved with the family is not how to prevent this crisis, but rather how to make it productive. The family is extremely vulnerable at this point and may be more susceptible to sensitive crisis intervention. Perhaps more concerned citizens and professionals might be willing to report suspected cases of sexual abuse if they were aware of the accompanying, underlying sense of relief members of the family may experience at the time of exposure. Social isolation occurs in these families almost without exception. The crisis period is a time when that isolation can be lessened by providing links to supportive services in the community.

Dispelling Myths with Facts

➤ The sex offender who victimizes children is far more often a member of the family or friend, rarely a stranger.

- Incest occurs within all socioeconomic classes. Incest does not occur only in very poor families as is commonly believed.
- The perpetrators of child sexual abuse are almost always male, rarely female.
- A child who reports sexual abuse should always be taken seriously.
- Victims of child sexual abuse are often blamed by the perpetrators and others for the incest. They are referred to as seductive and sexually precocious.
- Sexual abuse of males is usually initiated by the perpetrator before the child reaches puberty. Abuse of females may occur at any age, with a high percentage of assaults first occurring between the ages of five and nine.

Emotional or Mental Abuse

Characterized by any interaction with a child that damages self-esteem or psyche. Teasing, ridicule, and belittlement are common behaviors that are often damaging to children. Though most parents want "the best" for their child, unreasonable parental expectations can also be very destructive. Others who project their own personal needs, desires, and frustrations on their children may require them to "live out" parental fantasies of success and accomplishment.

Overprotective, dependent, or dictatorial caregivers can devastate a child. Parents who do not understand a youngster's developmental capabilities may inflict harsh criticism and/or punishment. Erratic and inconsistent discipline deprives the child of an important anchor needed for healthy development.

Emotional abuse is the most common kind of abuse inflicted on children by "well-meaning" parents. It may accompany other kinds of abuse and neglect.

Indicators of Emotional Abuse

Victims of emotional abuse may display symptoms of stress, often similar to those of physically or sexually abused children. The presence of the following behaviors, if not otherwise explainable, should be cause for investigation.

♦ Exhibits habit disorders, such as poor eye contact, sucking,

♦ biting, rocking enuresis, or eating and other food-related disorders

♦ Has conduct disorders, including withdrawal and anti-social behavior

♦ Has neurotic traits, such as sleeping disorders, inhibition of play, compulsive, hysteria, obsession, phobias, and hypochondria

♦ Is often suspicious, untrusting, pessimistic, depressed, anxious, preoccupied

♦ Demonstrates extreme behaviors, including overly compliant, passive, or extremely aggressive

♦ Has developmental lags in mental and emotional growth

♦ Attempts suicide

♦ Runs away

♦ Uses adaptive behavior in an attempt to respond to family's inconsistent interactions or expectations

♦ Demonstrates nervous tic, persistent stuttering, or speech disorder

Abuse by Siblings

Siblings play a larger role in a child's development than was once thought. A moderate amount of conflict among siblings is normal and useful for learning to interact and solve problems. However, violence, cruelty, or sexual exploitation by a sibling can have serious lasting consequences, as relationships among siblings form the model for relationships later in life. It is important for parents to show strong disapproval of abusive behavior and attempt to model healthy behavior. Though it may be impossible to control the actions of their children at all times, they can at least establish for all parties that there is a right and wrong way to interact.

Neglect

Defined as deprivation of proper nourishment, clothing, shelter, medical care, and/or nurturing, neglect is the most common form of child maltreatment. Neglected children are often left without proper discipline or supervision. Parents who neglect their child are often under tremendous stress. Typically they have poor coping and interactive skills. Many are barely able to support themselves and either cannot or choose not to give their children proper care. Because of an inability to communicate well with others, they often don't seek the help they need.

Difficulties in Defining Child Neglect

Developing a precise definition of neglect is not an easy task. In contrast to physical abuse, which usually has specific medical indicators such as bruises or broken bones and which occurs at a specific time, neglect may not produce visible signs, and occurs over a period of time. Neglect is usually a chronic failure to provide necessary physical and emotional support for a child. It is determined by a pattern of inattentive and/or dangerous child-rearing practices. But what does "chronic" mean? How long does it take to establish a pattern? What are dangerous child-rearing practices? The answers to these questions inevitably involve some degree of subjective judgment.

Community Standards

We can begin to answer these difficult questions by examining the child-rearing standards of the community. It can be said that neglect is seen by society as a deviant form of child-rearing which is unacceptable and harmful to a child, in contrast to those forms which are deemed growth-promoting and acceptable. Adequate and neglectful child-rearing are both socially defined terms. The dividing line between them may differ from one community to another and may change with time. Community A may condone certain child–rearing practices which Community B does not, or Community A may condemn today behaviors it deemed acceptable five years ago. While these flexible standards contribute to the difficulty of creating a single, universal definition of neglect, they indicate a basis from which we may approach the problem.

Physical Indicators of Neglect

♦ Consistent hunger, poor hygiene, and inappropriate dress
♦ Flattening of infant's head and bald spot on back of head
♦ Delayed mental or motor development
♦ Incessant crying or no crying at all (infants)
♦ Failure to attend school regularly
♦ Failure-to-thrive syndrome
♦ Persistent skin rashes, e.g., psoriasis, scabies, impetigo
♦ Excessive dental decay or gum disease
♦ Malnutrition and chronic anemia (in severe neglect – rickets, beriberi, and infantile scurvy)
♦ Ringworm, head or body lice, roach bite
♦ Weight loss with weight out of proportion to height
♦ Chronic or persistent digestive or intestinal disorders
♦ Is constantly fatigued, listless, or falls asleep in class

Behavioral indicators of neglect are often stress related and may be similar to those demonstrated by victims of other forms of abuse. As always, any behavior by a child that is a significant deviation from normal, is a cause for investigation.

What's the Difference Between Discipline and Abuse?

In properly applied discipline, both the parent and the child know and understand the desired outcome of any action taken. The parent tells the child or demonstrates the desired behavior in a positive, supportive way. The child may then be allowed to practice the behavior, receiving praise for attempts to achieve the goal set by the parent.

Parent/child interaction does not threaten either and allows both to express genuine feelings. Children can participate in making rules for the family, especially those that apply directly to him or her. Any failure to comply with rules has consistent, clearly defined, and appropriate consequences that help the child learn and grow.

Abuse is improperly applied punishment taken by the parent to vent anger, express negative thoughts about the child, and eliminate opportunity for the child to understand parental motives. Impulsive, inconsistent, or harsh behavior by the parent is perceived as condemnation by the child. The message received is usually one that convinces the victim that he or she is a "bad" person. Resentment, hostility, and thoughts of retaliation are often the result.

Parents who apply the same "discipline" for every infraction are not in tune with the child's needs and the result is that the disciplinary action is usually ineffective. This leads to frustration and may even frighten the parent when the child becomes resistant, or defiant. The result is an acceleration of parent/child misunderstanding, harsher punishment, and perhaps mutual distrust and hatred.

Parents who depend on corporal punishment to correct misbehaving children will find that as the child grows and becomes bigger and stronger, the spanking also must become stronger. The obvious result is that adolescents may be beaten as the only control the parent now has over the child. There are ways to rear children without sending the message that violence is normal behavior and the solution to problems between people.

Effective Parenting is the hardest job in the world

Even under ideal conditions, child rearing is a multi-faceted, complicated responsibility. Chronic stress, poverty, illness, emotional instability, and a myriad of other problems make it very difficult. The most effective parent, under severe stress, can lapse into a behavior that could be construed as abusive if he or she acted that way all the time. Abuse is defined as an action or lack of action that leaves emotional and physical scars on another person, especially a child. It would be unrealistic to try to determine whether a parent is abusive or not on the basis of one incident, unless that incident was dangerous or flagrantly serious.

What would be a minor incident to one person might be devastating to another. What makes the difference? Those children who are subjected to negative, demeaning, critical, blaming, or other esteem-damaging behaviors and who have no outlets for their negative feelings and no resources to help rebuild self-confidence and healthy self esteem are the most likely to suffer. Others who receive positive, constructive self-esteem messages from their parents or other adults, can cope with rare episodes of poor parenting.

Most parents are caring, positive, accepting, and patient with children who are learning about themselves and developing independence. Parents struggle with the "daily grind" of child-rearing and most of them do a remarkably good job. A good philosophy for parenting comes from this quote from Kahlil Gibran.

"Your children are not your children. They are the sons and daughters of life's longing for itself. They come through you, but not from you; and though they are with you, yet they belong not to you. You may give them your love, but not your thoughts; for they have their own thoughts. You may house their bodies, but not their souls, for their souls dwell in the house of tomorrow, which you cannot visit; not even in your dreams. You may strive to be like them, but seek not to make them like you."

Not All Children with Behavior Problems are Abused Children.

More Facts About Abused Children

- In the United States, there are almost one million cases of child abuse each year.
- Over one thousand children die each year from child abuse.
- Neglect is the most common type of child abuse, but you don't hear much about it because the wounds and scars of neglect are not always easily seen.
- Almost nine of ten abusers are the children's own parents.
- Good news! Victims and their families can get help and successfully overcome abuse.

Behavioral Indicators of Abusive Parents

- Show little concern for their child's problems
- Take an unusual amount of time to seek health care for the
- child
- Do not adequately explain an injury
- Are reluctant to share information about the child with teachers or health care professionals
- Misusing drugs or alcohol
- Child is described as "bad" by parents
- Have no one to turn to in crisis
- Have excessive and unrealistic expectations for the child
- Are overly strict disciplinarians
- Consistently not in control of their own emotions
- Are unusually antagonistic and hostile when talking about the child's health problems.

Signs or indicators of abuse may come from the child or from the parent. It is important to consider the whole picture of a family's well being, rather than one single indicator. If there are significant indicators of abuse that are not clearly explainable by another cause, abuse should be suspected and the suspicions reported to the proper authority.

What Can Be Done about Child Abuse?

Children who have been abused and their families need help. Proper intervention depends on the severity of the abuse and the resources available. Anyone who is being abused or suspects that someone else is being abused should report it to the proper authorities.

Reporting suspected abuse can help families break the cycle of abusive behavior. Many times the reporter is afraid to "interfere" or "meddle" in situations not directly affecting his or her own life. Some people think that they must prove the abuse in order to report it. Not so. The task of proving whether or not child abuse is occurring is up to the state or local authorities.

Many times when investigations are made, suspected abuse is not actually occurring but the intervention by a case worker can be beneficial to the family in question. Information about community resources, support groups, classes and other helpful tips can help families relieve stress and learn better ways of coping with problems. If abuse is occurring, the visit may trigger action on the part of the parents to get help. Case workers may determine that minimal intervention is necessary and families willing to seek counseling can develop new, healthy relationships.

In the most severe cases, children may need to be removed from the home to protect them from further harm, though this occurs in a very small minority of reported cases. Perpetrators may be arrested and jailed. When this happens the fate of the family is usually up to the courts. Children may be permanently removed from the home and the abusers sent to prison.

Receiving a Disclosure

According to Grace Y. Miller, the Child Abuse and Neglect Truancy Officer for Broward County, Florida school system, a disclosure may or may not be intentional. Regardless of the intent, there are a number of things to keep in mind during the discussion phase:

1.   Believe what the child has told you.

2. Tell the child that you are glad he/she has informed you, and let the child know that you are sorry about what happened.

3. Be aware of your feelings during the disclosure, as children are sensitive to them at this time. Do not communicate feelings of horror, repugnance, or fright to the child. Your being quietly confident and comfortable are what the child needs most.

4. Allow the child to tell you about what happened in a free and open manner. Let them proceed at their own pace, using language that is comfortable.

5. Unless you are specifically trained for this work, do not "interview" the child but arrange for the involvement of a professional.

6. The child may feel guilty and need your reassurance that the abuse was not his/her fault. Tell them that it's not their fault. It's always the older person's fault.

7. If it is incest being disclosed, any comments suggesting that he/she might be fabricating the story will activate fears of not being believed, and the child may choose to become silent. The abuser may have overtly or covertly threatened the child to remain silent.

8. Explain to the child that you are required to report it. State that the purpose of reporting is to get help for the family from people who work with this kind of problem so that it doesn't occur again.

9. Make no promises or guarantees to the child that are beyond your control. Don't promise to keep it a "secret."

Statistics

Statistics released by the U.S. Department of Health and Human Services in April of 2002 reveal the following about reported child abuse and neglect cases in America in the year 2000:

Victims

- There were 879,000 confirmed cases of child maltreatment, a rate of 12.2 cases per 1,000 children, out of approximately three million reports of suspected maltreatment.

- The rate of confirmed cases peaked in 1993 at 15.3 cases per 1,000, and had fallen every year until 1999 when it was 11.8.

- Approximately 1,200 children (23 children per week) died of abuse or neglect. Children under age one accounted for 44% of child fatalities and 85% of the total were under age six.

- The confirmed reports of maltreatment were categorized as follows: 62% suffered neglect, 19% suffered physical abuse, 10% were sexually abused, and eight percent were psychologically mistreated. 84% of victims were abused by a parent. The likelihood of becoming a victim of abuse decreased with age. Infants, from birth to age three, experienced a rate of 15.7 cases per 1,000, while for 16 and 17 year olds, the rate was 5.7 per 1,000 children of the same age.

- Victimization rates were only slightly higher for girls (12.8 per 1,000) than boys (11.2 per 1,000) except in the case of sexual abuse. In this case, the rate was 1.7 per 1,000 for girls and .4 per 1,000 for boys.

- 51% of victims were White, 25% were African American, 15% were Hispanic, American Indian/Alaska Native accounted for 2%, and Asian/Pacific Islanders accounted for 1%.

(Due to missing data, the total is less than 100%).

Perpetrators

- Perpetrators of child abuse and neglect, normally defined as parents, relatives, baby-sitters, foster parents and other caregivers who have maltreated a child, break down as follows: 60% female, 40% male. The median age for females was 31 years, while the median for males was 34.

- Mothers acting alone were responsible for 47% of neglect victims, and 32 % of physical abuse victims. In the case of sexual abuse, non-relatives were responsible for 29% of victims, fathers acting alone accounted for 22% and other relatives were responsible for 19%.

Non-Intentional Physical Abuse

Not all child abuse is intentional. Parents who refrain from such behaviors as hitting their child may inflict injury without meaning to. Non-intentional physical abuse includes such behaviors as shaking, tossing, throwing, and grabbing.

> ### Shaking of Children is a Leading Cause of Retardation and Death in Children up to Six Years of Age

Many parents frustrated by their child's inattention, shake the child as a means of getting his attention. These parents are shocked when told that the shaking of infants and small children is one of the leading causes of death and retardation in the United States.

The shaking of a human body, including the head, causes the brain to strike repeatedly the inside of the skull, thus causing bilateral subdural hematomas (bruises to the brain). The swelling caused by the hematoma causes pressure on various parts of the brain, which may cause temporary or permanent brain damage, retardation, paralysis or death. *Infants are extremely vulnerable to this type of injury.*

As children grow and develop, parents enjoy their giggles as they toss their children up in the air and catch them over and over again. The danger of a child's head hitting the ceiling or the child being dropped and injured, are obvious. The danger of a child's brain repeatedly impacting against the inside of the skull does not occur to most parents.

Teen/Single Parents

The children of young and single women are especially vulnerable to abuse. It may be at the hands of a frustrated, scared, and lonely parent, or a boyfriend or other relation who has come into the life of the small family. The stresses the mother may experience could be beyond anything she imagined before making a decision to have a child.

To bring another person into the world is the most important thing that most of us will ever do. To provide for a child, to protect them against harm, and to nurture them to adulthood, are tasks requiring a great deal of work, patience, self-sacrifice, maturity, and a sense of humor. Love alone is not enough. Being a parent is a lot about giving and not much about getting back. There is little question that the best environment for raising children is that of a stable, loving marriage, preferably with relatives and adult friends offering support.

Some young women find themselves having children without these assets and attributes. It's important for them to know that they, too, can be great parents! Patience, self-sacrifice and even a sense of humor can be learned while maturity will follow in time. Good friends with shared interests can be found.

Young parents will have to overcome many challenges but help is there if they look for it, and the goal of raising a healthy happy child can be attained by any parent willing to work hard at it.

Becoming a Parent is a Commitment for Life.

Chapter 7

You Must Report Child Abuse

> Reporting suspected abuse is the first and foremost thing
> one can do to stop child abuse. Anyone who suspects child
> abuse is ethically obligated to report it and in some cases
> legally required to report it.

Any professional, such as a teacher or doctor, who fails to
report abuse or knowingly prevents another from doing so may
be liable for prosecution.

Some professionals have additional responsibilities. For
example, the law gives enforcement officers, physicians, and
persons in charge of hospitals or similar institutions, the
authority to take a child into protective custody if that child
appears to be in imminent danger. These professionals may
authorize X-ray examination of a child without the consent of
the parents or legal guardians if he or she has cause to suspect
that an injury was the result of child abuse.

> Those who report child abuse are protected in two ways—
> immunity from liability and confidentiality.

Anyone making a report "in good faith" is specifically
immune from any civil or criminal charges that might result.
Any person may report suspected cases of child abuse or neglect
anonymously. However, professionals are encouraged to give
their names to speed the investigation of abuse. The
professional is also urged to inform the family that he or she is

obligated by law to make a report, while stressing continuing support and concern for the family.

To Report Abuse or Neglect the Following Information is Important

1. Name and address of child and parent or guardian, if known.
2. Child's age and siblings' names and ages, if known.
3. Nature and extent of alleged abuse or neglect.
4. Identity of abuser, if known.
5. Name of person reporting, if desired.
6. Other information the reporter believes would be helpful in establishing cause of injury or neglect.

When a report is made an investigation follows to determine its validity. There is contact with the parents to evaluate the risk of further injury to the child while in the home. Identification will be made of the family problems that contributed to the abuse or neglect in order to determine the potential for treatment. A plan to stabilize and rehabilitate the family using state and community services will then be drawn up.

The highest priority in all cases of abuse and neglect is to protect the child.

If in doubt, the issue should be resolved in favor of the child. The second priority of treatment is to help the parents. The third priority is to restore the family if possible. Most children are too young or too frightened to report their abuse or neglect themselves. No child should ever be held accountable for the actions of an adult. It is never the child's fault.

Don't give up—be persistent! The few minutes it may take are not nearly so precious as the life you may save.

Often we become frustrated when we encounter the red tape of bureaucracy. Having made up your mind to place that all-important call, don't give up when you find yourself shuttled from one person to another. Instead, think of the life and future of the child.

If you are in a position to offer ongoing support to the victim or the family, do so. Healthy relationships are vital to minimizing the harm that stems from abuse and building constructive feelings and attitudes.

How Does the System Work?

The name of the state agency charged with protecting children varies from state-to-state. In many states, it is the Department of Children and Families (DCF). In some states, private agencies are being given some of the work formerly done by DCF, in an effort to improve the responsiveness of the service. DCF usually conducts investigations of reported cases of child abuse and neglect, though in some cases law enforcement personnel with special training are involved. If a case is considered valid or "founded," DCF makes a plan for intervention. They are required to intervene to "support, maintain, and strengthen family ties" and may ask for the voluntary cooperation of the parents. Removal of a child from his or her family is a last resort and only occurs in a very small percent of the cases.

DCF can pursue court action when the family's voluntary cooperation is not obtained. DCF may present testimony and ask a judge to adjudicate the child as "dependent." This legal determination gives the state the authority to mandate Protective Supervision of a family or place a child in DCF custody.

If a family is "under DCF Protective Services," the child remains in the home, and a case worker is assigned to supervise the home situation. When a child is removed, the DCF/Child Welfare Unit places the child in foster care and files a written plan for the parents to work toward the return of the child.

A Guardian Ad Litem may be appointed by the court to conduct an independent investigation of the case, advocate in the child's best interest, and make a recommendation to the court on disposition. The guardian may be a trained lay person or an attorney who has a legal mandate for action. The Guardian Ad Litem (GAL) may visit the school to review records and talk with the child's teachers. The GAL will have a written order from the court authorizing the school to release information.

What Can You Do To Help?

There are probably organizations in your community doing excellent work to stop abuse. Many or most are under funded and understaffed. Consider volunteering your time and efforts with one of these groups. If there is a need not being met in your community, consider starting a group to address it.

The following are key areas of need:

Guardians Ad Litem: These volunteers are a vital support for children involved with the system. In many communities, average citizens can perform this valuable service. Make a call.

Parent Training Programs: Classes and/or support groups in which parents or expectant parents can practice nurturing techniques, positive approaches to parenting and learn more about their own styles of child rearing.

Parent Support Groups: Peer groups in which parents can work out frustrations, share problems, and compare techniques with others. Peer support is a very effective tool in helping parents learn new methods of parenting.

Support Services for Parents of "Special Needs" Children: Groups in which parents can process problem-solving techniques, share information, and feelings about the stressful job of rearing disabled, chronically ill, retarded or otherwise debilitated children.

Home Visitor Assistance Programs: Professionals or trained volunteers can provide in-home assistance to young parents, single parents, or others with needs beyond their abilities or resources. Home visitors provide support, effective modeling of parenting techniques, information about community resources, a friendly ear to listen to parental concerns.

Crisis Services 24 Hours a day: Nursery facilities for children at risk. The children can stay in a warm, nurturing environment while parents solve problems that may be causing them to be abusive. The nursery can also serve as a place for children who are waiting for foster homes.

Respite Care: Temporary services offered at low or no cost to parents who may need to attend to personal or family needs, as "time out" for overworked parents or caregivers.

Mental Health Services: Available to anyone who is experiencing personal crisis. The facility should have a professional staff qualified to deal with potential suicide or other possibly dangerous situations. Clients may be kept overnight or until they can be admitted to a hospital for more intensive care, or are referred to a mental health therapist.

Community Hotlines/Warmlines: To give support and information to parents and provide a confidential, reassuring source of help for children who need to talk about problems. It can also be an after-school service to provide children with a source of reassurance and help. This program would only need to be in operation for a few hours during the day.

Treatment Programs: Therapy programs for children, abusers, and adult victims who have never resolved the issues related to their victimization as children. It can also provide family therapy to maintain family integrity and improve relationships.

School Programs: Curriculum development – self-esteem building programs, teaching personal responsibility and respect for self and others. Prevention for students - how to avoid abusive situations and what to do if already being abused. Groups for victims—peer groups for students who have been abused or threatened with abuse. In-service for all staff; recognition of signs and symptoms, and how to intervene properly and how to report suspected abuse.

Spouse Abuse Shelter—Domestic Violence Shelter: Emergency housing and treatment for those who have been battered or otherwise abused. Services include a nursery and a school for children who come to the shelter with a parent.

Neighborhood Prevention Programs: Friends and neighbors can cooperate to create very effective prevention programs. An example is the Neighborhood Watch Program. Other efforts can include the development of childcare cooperatives where parents can exchange babysitting duties with other parents, creating time for social and recreational activities.

Neighborhood associations can identify "safe" homes where children could stay on the way home from school if they felt threatened. Parents can volunteer time to be crossing guards during preschool and after-school hours. Playgrounds can be supervised by older children or designated parents. Children need to be taught to recognize and avoid potentially dangerous situations. They also can learn how and where to get help in an emergency.

Prevention in the Home: Any member of the family can act to improve the family situation. Parents can get marital counseling or family counseling to help improve relationships. Children who feel threatened or abused can report the abuse to someone at school or in the neighborhood so that a report can be made to the authorities.

Many times the people who need help most are the least likely to ask for it. Victims sometimes feel that any effort would be useless, that nobody would believe them any way. Fear, guilt and anxiety keep many people imprisoned in situations that could be improved with a minimum of effort.

Guidelines for Interactions within Families

➤ Consideration for each member of the family as an individual with basic human rights.

➤ Acceptance of differences in personal priorities within legal and moral guidelines.

➤ Empathetic treatment of those who experience frustration anger and failure.

➤ Caring for each other without trying to force change.

➤ Honesty in interpersonal communication and transactions.

- Awareness of one's own feelings and developing the ability to sense the true feelings of others.
- Improve communications within the family by becoming an "active listener."
- Family meetings to discuss schedules, business, and other planning.
- Assignment of duties, chores, and responsibilities so that no one is unfairly burdened.
- Have fun together as a family.
- Laugh with each other, not at each other.
- Share personal triumphs as well as problems.

Developing A Prevention Program

Schools are using a variety of presentations with children. Films and videotapes are available through DCF. Generally, presentations, whether one-time or done as a series of planned discussions, have the following messages in common:

- A discussion of the continuum of touching from good to bad, including both sexually and physically abusive touches.
- A right to control access to one's own body, with discussion of appropriate exceptions (e.g. medical exams, bathing).
- An encouragement of children to trust their own feelings to recognize situations in which they are being treated inappropriately.
- An emphasis on saying "no" to abuse in a variety of ways.
- Instructions to "tell" and identification of support systems.

What More Can You Do to Help?

Plenty! Begin by learning about the dynamics of abuse. Being well informed is mandatory if one is to be effective in the fight against child abuse. Learn about community resources. What are the most pressing needs? Meet the people who are already working on the problems of abuse and offer to help.

Major problems are not addressed because most law-makers do not realize the magnitude of the problem or are not informed enough to establish effective prevention programs. Write them. Telephone them. Take them to lunch. Inform them of the needs!

Anyone wanting to make a difference, can.

Depending upon personal resources, a person can make donations to prevention programs or offer their time. Social service agencies need well-trained, educated, experienced personnel to administer effective programs but most cannot pay competitive wages.

State and local child protective services often have trouble in recruiting, hiring, placing, and keeping experienced people because of low pay scales. This is sometimes referred to as the revolving door syndrome—no sooner than people train and learn their jobs, they find better-paying positions elsewhere. Case loads build up, people work too much overtime, and burnout causes people to make mistakes, and develop apathetic attitudes and quit.

➢ Volunteer time and encourage others to do the same. Volunteerism is the backbone of many successful services to families. Research community volunteer placements and decide where help is needed most. It is important that volunteers be screened, trained, and placed in jobs that they are suited for and enjoy.

➢ Organize neighborhood residents to be aware of any problems and find appropriate solutions to them. If there are children who seem to need help, report it to the local authorities. Help neighbors learn to network and share information and resources.

➢ Patronize only certified day care centers which screen and hire qualified personnel. Check references for babysitters and warn others of problems with any particular sitter.

➢ Apply for a license to be a foster parent. There is a critical shortage of suitable placement homes for children who have been removed from their homes. This has proved to be a very rewarding venture for many people.

124

- ➢ Attend parenting classes to see how personal practices can be modified or improved. Meet new people and compare solutions to any problems with child rearing. Assess personal relationships for any negative, hurtful, and chronic situations which may need to be changed.
- ➢ Make a home telephone directory which includes numbers of friends, coworkers, neighbors, repair services, maintenance people, and emergency services. Teach children to use it.
- ➢ Volunteer to work in schools as a teacher's aide, clinic attendant, or office worker. Determine the school policy on child abuse and, if necessary, insist that the faculty and administrators receive child abuse in-service training.
- ➢ Check out any situations involving rumors of child abuse or neglect in your community. Investigate recreational programs involving children and insist that personnel be screened thoroughly.
- ➢ Assist in organizing and operating church programs that offer services to the poor. Food, clothing and resource information can be a welcome offering to a family in need.
- ➢ Start a "latchkey" program for children whose parents must work and cannot be at home to supervise them after school and in the summer when school is out.
- ➢ Visit local facilities that provide residential services to abused or homeless children. Ask about policies regarding discipline and staff qualifications and training. Offer assistance in performing needed tasks. Make friends with children and include them in family outings.
- ➢ Teen pregnancy has become a major problem in most parts or our country. Many communities do not have adequate prevention programs that provide necessary information about the problems to teens. Prenatal health care programs are needed for those who can not afford proper care.
- ➢ Alternative programs for school dropouts are needed to give them an opportunity to learn a skill or trade. These programs need to address the child as a person with special needs and problems. They need effective counseling and follow-up.

125

- ➢ Support local drug and alcohol abuse prevention programs. Learn about substance abuse and its effects on families.
- ➢ If your community does not have a spouse abuse (domestic violence) shelter, learn what is needed to start one.
- ➢ Write grants to secure funding for crisis services if they are not available in the community.

There are hundreds of ways that one person can help stop child abuse—recognizing problems, creating awareness, and taking personal responsibility for one's own actions.

The most important personal contribution is for each person to learn to nurture and love their own family members. Create time for families to be together when the television is off and the radio is not blaring and let each family member talk about what interest them. Learn to praise children for what they do right and convert criticism into caring assistance.

Ursula Sunshine was only one among thousands of children who desperately needed help to escape the ravages of child abuse. Hers was one of the worst cases. It began with an emotionally dependent parent who had been a victim herself, and ended in the child's tormented death.

Not all cases of child abuse are this gruesome. Many are much more subtle and harder to identify. If no one heard Ursula in her grim struggle for help, who will hear the other children crying for help now?

The Worst Thing You Can Do About Child Abuse is Nothing!

Organizations That Can Help
(For more resources go to *www.deathfromchildabuse.com*)

PARENTS ANONYMOUS – With 35 organizations in 24 states, PA is a self-help organization that works towards stopping the abuse cycle. They have meetings, hotlines and mutual support programs. They also publish a newsletter and maintain an information service.

www.parentsanonymous.org
909-621-6184

CHILD WELFARE LEAGUE OF AMERICA, INC. is an organization to promote the well-being of all children and their families. It gives priority to the unmet needs of children lacking physical, emotional and intellectual care and nurturing. Their goal is to strengthen delivery of services: to formulate, promote and advocate public policies that benefit children and their families.

www.cwla.org
440 1st St. N.W., Third Floor , Washington, DC 20001
202-638-2952

NATIONAL CLEARINGHOUSE ON CHILD ABUSE AND NEGLECT INFORMATION provides information and expertise on improving the prevention, identification and treatment of child abuse and neglect. Databases describing ongoing research programs, abstracts of public documents, excerpts of state child abuse laws, a listing of available publications, directories and audiovisual materials are available.

www.calib.com/nccanch
P.O. Box 1182, Washington, D.C. 20013
1-800-FYI-3366
703-385-7565

CHILDHELP USA operates a NATIONAL CHILD ABUSE HOTLINE providing crisis counseling, information and referral from a professionally trained staff of counselors.

www.childhelpusa.org
P.O. Box 630, Hollywood, CA 90028
1-800-4-A-CHILD

PREVENT CHILD ABUSE AMERICA is the leading organization working at the national, state and local levels to prevent the abuse and neglect of our nation's children. The organization is known for its prevention programs, public awareness initiatives and research.

www.preventchildabuse.org
200 S. Michigan Avenue, Chicago, IL 60604
1-800-CHILDREN

KEMPE CHILDREN'S CENTER was established in 1972 to provide a clinically based resource for training, consultation , research and program development on all forms of abuse and neglect. Through multidisciplinary approaches, the center focuses on improving the recognition, treatment and prevention of abuse and neglect.

www.kempecenter.org/
1825 Marion St., Denver, CO 80218
303-864-5252

THE NATIONAL CENTER FOR MISSING AND EXPLOITED CHILDREN serves as a clearinghouse of information on missing or exploited children; provides technical assistance to citizens and law enforcement agencies; offers training programs to schools and law enforcement; distributes photos and descriptions of missing children nationwide; coordinates a speakers bureau; provides information and advice on effective state legislation related to the safety and protection of children and maintains 15 toll-free hotlines covering the United States and Canada.

www.missingkids.com
699 Prince St., Alexandria, VA 22314
1-800-843-5678

AMERICAN ASSOCIATION FOR PROTECTING CHILDREN
(A division of the American Humane Association) is a national resource center for child abuse and neglect that provides training, program evaluation and state by state reporting statistics.

www.americanhumane.org/cpmain.html
www.children@americanhumane.org
1-800-227-4645

CHILD CARE AWARE. Contact Child Care Aware and find the Child Care Resource & Referral agency serving you area. In additional, you will find other valuable information regarding quality child care.

www.ChildCareAware.org
1-800-424-2246

FOR KIDS SAKE is a 28 year old child abuse prevention agency providing mobile outreach, assessment and intake to the hardest to serve children and their families located in low income and rural neighborhoods. For Kids Sake's goal include developing and identifying and provide services that aid in breaking the intergenerational cycle of child abuse; promotes and provides services which support families (natural, adoptive, or foster) in developing positive parenting and health practices.

www.ForKidsSake.org
351 Old Newport Blvd. #344
Newport Beach, CA 92663
924-293-4004

NATIONAL RUNAWAY SWITCHBOARD Every day 1.3 million runaway and homeless youth live on the streets of America. Each year approximately 5,000 runaway and homeless youth die from assault illness, suicide. (source: National Runaway Switchboard

www.nrscrisisline.org
1-800-621-4000

Chapter 8

Domestic Violence

(The following information on Domestic Violence was provided courtesy of Jonathan H. Vanden, a case manager at The Spring of Tampa Bay. Since 1977, The Spring has provided refuge to over 24,000 victims and their dependent children. As the largest of Florida's 38 certified centers, The Spring offers clients the services they need to rebuild their lives. Crisis counselors answer hotline calls and admit shelter clients 24 hours a day, 365 days a year. A K-8 public school provides safe, quality schooling for children living in a domestic violence shelter. Education and employment counseling help victims restore their self-esteem and independence. Licensed, NAEYC-accredited childcare facilities are available for working parents, as well as after–school programs for children. Transitional housing allows clients to pursue their educational or vocational goals for up to two years. Through direct service, community education, and intervention, The Spring strives to break the cycle of violence and restore peace to violent families.)

What is Domestic Violence?

Domestic violence occurs when a pattern of abusive, violent, and controlling behaviors exist between two or more people involved in a close or intimate relationship. Domestic violence exists between family members, between friends, and between intimates or partners. Domestic violence can affect people from all walks of life, no-matter their age, gender, race, religion, social class, or sexual preference.

Child abuse is a common form of domestic violence, one in which the victim is a child. Though the term domestic violence, is usually applied to behavior among adults, to a large extent, the causes and underlying motivations are the same. Child abuse and domestic violence are often found in the same families.

130

Physical Abuse

Physical abuse occurs when the abuser purposely hurts the victim's body with their body or a weapon. Examples of this type of abuse would be hitting, kicking, punching, slapping, burning, biting, throwing or striking the victim with a hard or dangerous object, etc.

Psychological Abuse
(Mental / Emotional Abuse)

Psychological abuse takes place when the abuser, as part of a behavior pattern, purposely hurts the feelings or disregards the emotional well being of the victim. Actions such as name calling, using insults, making threats of physical or emotional harm, forcing the victim to do things that are humiliating and degrading are examples of psychological abuse.

Sexual Abuse

Sexual abuse can be described as any unwanted and/or harmful sexual behavior. That activity may result from violent coercion, but is often the result of emotional manipulation, even psychological blackmail on the part of the perpetrator. Counselors or other trusted individuals can help if they are told.

Money as a Weapon

It is not unusual for an abuser to keep control of the victim by keeping the victim from having control over their money or finances. A victim of "economic" abuse might not be allowed to work, forced to stop work, made to ask or beg for money, forced to work and not have control over their earnings, or given inadequate allowances of money for personal or family needs. Keeping the victim financially dependent is a common strategy for preventing that person from leaving the relationship.

The elderly are particularly vulnerable to loss of control of their financial life and in extreme cases, having their money stolen from them by abusive family members or acquaintances.

Domestic Violence – How Does it Start?

A person who has been abused in a domestic violence situation, whether as a child or an adult, is more likely to become either a future abuser or victim. Domestic Violence often carries over from generation to generation because abuse is a learned behavior. The longer a person is exposed to an abusive situation, the more likely they are to see their abuse as "normal" or what they deserve. If a person is unable to identify that abuse exists, as they continue throughout their life, they are more likely to identify actions or behaviors that are abusive as normal and even loving. Further, they are more likely to repeat the cycle of Domestic Violence, either as abuser or victim and pass it on to their children.

How Can We Stop Abuse and Avoid a Domestic Violence Situation?

Often the parties in an abusive relationship fail to recognize the roles they are playing. The following are warning signs for both the victim and the abuser, that help may be needed. Any one sign is cause for concern. Two or more signs or an episode of violence are a warning to get help immediately. It is sometimes difficult for people to recognize that they are in an abusive relationship. There are tools that can be helpful in identifying abusive unhealthy behaviors. Check out the following 16 Warning Signs of an Abusive Relationship:

16 Warning Signs of Domestic Violence

(The following is an adapted version of the 16 Warning Signs of Domestic Violence by Lydia Walker)

1. Is jealous and possessive
2. Tries to control your life
3. Has unrealistic expectations
4. Isolates you from friends and family
5. Blames others for their problems and mistakes
6. Makes everyone else responsible for their feelings
7. Says their feelings are easily hurt

8. Is cruel to animals and children
9. Uses force during sex
10. Yells and calls you names
11. Pushes for a quick relationship
12. Demands rigid sex roles
13. Has sudden mood swings
14. Has a history of battering
15. Threatens violence to you, your loved ones, pets, etc.
16. Threatens to reveal personal or damaging information about you to your family or employer

---

Don't Wait - Get Help Now!

Victim Services

Hotlines offer over-the-phone counseling, information and referrals to places that can help.

Support/Outreach Centers offer one on one counseling, group counseling, legal advice and safety advice.

Emergency Shelters offer emergency shelter or housing with onsite counseling and support services.

Crisis/Mental Health Centers offer support for individuals in crisis who are in need of immediate intervention.

Abuser Services

Outreach offers anger management classes, batterer intervention programs, group counseling, and individual counseling.

Crisis/Mental Health Centers offer support for individuals in crisis who are in need of immediate intervention.

To find the resource service nearest you, call the toll free number to the **National Domestic Violence Hotline 1-800-799-SAFE (7233)**. All calls are confidential, if you are not sure what type of service you are looking for, do not be afraid or embarrassed to explain your situation. The Crisis Counselors that answer the phones are trained professionals who can assist you in finding the services that will best suit your needs.

If you need immediate assistance, dial 911.

Plan for Personal Safety
Signs of Danger

Anyone who has experienced abuse needs to know that any of the following means their situation is becoming more dangerous:

- ✓ Abuse gets rougher
- ✓ There is a gun in the house
- ✓ Abuser uses drugs such as cocaine or heroin
- ✓ Abuser threatens to kill others
- ✓ Abuser talks about suicide
- ✓ Abuser is drunk often
- ✓ Abuser hits you in front of other people
- ✓ Abuser hurts or kills animals

If You Are Abused, What Are Your Options?

- ✓ Call the police in an emergency.
- ✓ File a police report about the violence.
- ✓ Have the abuser ordered by the court to stay away from you by getting an Injunction for Protection.
- ✓ See a doctor for injuries (ask him/her to document the injuries).
- ✓ Document the abuse, get pictures.
- ✓ Talk to a friend, family member, neighbor or someone else for support and ask for help.
- ✓ Call a domestic violence shelter to talk, get information or ideas or make a safety or escape plan.
- ✓ Insist that perpetrator enter a batterer intervention program.

If You Know of Someone Being Abused, Don't Look the Other Way

Let them know that you are concerned and offer to listen. Respect their choices, but encourage them to talk with professionals about safety issues. Offer as much help as you can, but don't take risks with your own safety. Some examples of ways you can help are: providing childcare, transportation, a place to stay, a job or lending them money.

> **Your support and encouragement can be of tremendous value to a friend, neighbor or family member.**

Dating Violence

What is Dating Violence?

Dating Violence occurs when one partner abuses the other in a dating relationship. Abuse includes any words or actions meant to control or hurt another person.

Dating violence is very common. Chances are, someone you know has been the victim of dating violence. Men and women may both initiate violence in relationships, but women are much more likely to experience physical or emotional harm.

Dating Violence can have serious effects which may include:

✓ Physical injuries, such as bruises and broken bones
✓ Emotional problems, such as low self-esteem
✓ Death

Healthy Relationships

You and your partner feel good about each other and the relationship

✓ You treat one another with respect and courtesy
✓ You communicate clearly and let one another know what each of you really thinks
✓ You feel free to question each other and explore problems
✓ You accept that even healthy relationships don't always work out

There are Different Forms of Dating Violence

Emotional Abuse – Harming a person's self esteem

✓ Repeated lies and broken promises
✓ Withholding affection—giving the "silent treatment"
✓ Extreme jealousy that keeps a partner away from family, friends or interests
✓ Insults and put-downs
✓ Threats
✓ Controlling a person's every move—how to dress, what to eat, where to go, etc.

Physical Abuse -Causing physical pain or injury

✓ Punching, kicking, shaking, slapping or restraining someone
✓ Attacking with a weapon
✓ Tickling or hugging if it's unwanted

Sexual Abuse – Any kind of unwanted sexual advance or contact. It can include everything from unwelcome sexual comments to kissing to intercourse.

Forced sex between two people who know each other is called acquaintance rape or date rape. It is a common and serious problem, and it's a crime!

You Always Have the Right to Say No to Sex.

This is true even if you've agreed to sex before. You don't owe your date sex or anything else just because you went out with him or her or did something special that evening.

Some people feel that an unhealthy relationship is better than none at all, but it's not. In fact, it can be very dangerous.

Abusers often blame the other person for "causing" the abuse. This is not true. It's the abuser who needs to change his or her behavior.

Abusers often regret their actions and apologize. But before long, they abuse again. Abuse usually gets worse rather than better. If you are being abused, don't think that apologies, promises or kind treatment following abuse means it won't happen again.

Characteristics of Acquaintance or Date Rapists

(From Avoiding Rape On and Off Campus, Second Edition, by Carol Pritchard)

- Acts immaturely, shows little empathy or feeling for others and displays little social conscience.
- Displays anger or aggression either verbally or physically. May be displayed during conversations by general negative references to women, vulgarity, curtness toward others, and the like. Often views women as adversaries.
- Acts "macho" and discusses acts of physical prowess excessively.
- Displays short temper, physically abusive (slapping, grabbing arms, etc.).
- Acts excessively jealous and/or possessive of you. Be especially suspicious of this behavior if you have recently met or are on a first or second date.
- Ignores your space boundaries by being too close or by placing his hand on your thigh, etc. especially in public.
- Ignores your wishes.

137

- Attempts to make you feel guilty or accuses you of being "uptight."
- Becomes hostile and/or increasingly more aggressive when you say no about anything.
- Insists on being alone with you on a first date.
- Demands your attention or compliance at inappropriate times such as during a class.
- Asks personal questions and is interested in knowing more than you want to tell him.
- Subscribes excessively to traditional male and female stereotypes.

You Can Reduce the Risk of Dating Violence

Communicate Clearly and let your partner know you will not tolerate any abuse. Also discuss sexual boundaries before a situation arises.

Stay in Control of what is happening to you. Don't use alcohol or other drugs. Have your own way home in case you need it. Always carry change for a pay phone.

Avoid Isolated Places, especially until you get to know the other person. Stay away from places where you'll be alone.

Trust Your Instincts if you have concerns about a potential date. Get to know the person before going out, or go out with a group.

Avoid People with Overly Possessive and Excessively Jealous Behavior. They are not indicators of great love. They are potentially dangerous and will stifle your happiness. Don't be flattered by the "attention". Get away from it.

Be Choosy and Avoid Dating People Who:

- Put down others often
- Use alcohol or other drugs
- Want to be in control of everything
- Have angry outbursts or are extremely jealous
- Use physical force
- Drive recklessly or drink and drive

You Can End an Unhealthy Relationship

Believe in yourself and stand by your feelings. If you feel you were abused, talk to someone you can trust.

Get out. Abusive relationships usually get worse, not better. Make sure you're safe, and resist the temptation to give the person one more chance.

Get Help

- **If you've been physically harmed, get medical attention.**

- **If you fear you are in danger, seek shelter and call the police.**

- **Talk with a friend, crisis hotline, mental health center or member of the clergy.**

- **Consider counseling, even if the abuse happened long ago.**

If You Know a Victim of Dating Violence

- **Believe and support the person.**

- **Encourage the victim to get help and get out of the relationship.**

Abuse is Never the Victim's Fault

What's In Store for the Future?

In the years since the murder of Ursula Sunshine Assaid and the telling of her story, much has changed. Public awareness, through education, the media, and stories like Ursula's, has greatly improved. Much of the public is less tolerant of abusive behavior in their families and neighborhoods, and they know more about how to stop it. Parents are replacing antiquated child-rearing tactics with effective and humane methods of guidance and instruction that motivate rather than cripple. For many, the "time-out" has replaced the "spanking". Many school systems have stepped up, recognizing that they have a unique role to play, and made the teaching of "relationship skills" a priority. And most importantly, individuals, whether abuse victims or not, are making the conscious decision every day to deny their darker, more fearful impulses, and celebrate love and acceptance in their families and relationships and expect the same in return.

The statistics show us that it is getting better. They also show how very far we have to go until cruelty, exploitation and neglect are rare aberrant acts rather than everyday events. Over three deaths every day from child abuse and neglect are the frightening tip of a huge and dangerous iceberg. The cost of abuse in human potential is almost unimaginable. The cost in dollars could be calculated, and it would run to the many tens of billions every year.

Individuals like you make the difference. We can't expect schools, law enforcement, and social service agencies to raise our children or bring peace to our lives. The best efforts by dedicated caring professionals in government and private organizations cannot replace the power of individuals to teach and practice love, tolerance, wisdom and humor in day-to-day life.